descartes

D1570789

The *Blackwell Great Minds* series gives readers a strong sense of the fundamental views of the great western philosophers and captures the relevance of these philosophers to the way we think and live today.

1. Kant by Allen W. Wood
2. Augustine by Gareth B. Matthews
3. Descartes by André Gombay

Forthcoming
Aristotle by Jennifer Whiting
Nietzsche by Richard Schacht
Plato by Paul Woodruff
Sartre by Katherine J. Morris
Spinoza by Don Garrett
Wittgenstein by Hans Sluga
Schopenhauer by Robert Wicks
Heidegger by Taylor Carman
Maimonides by Tamar Rudavsky
Darwin by Michael Ruse

blackwell great minds

edited by Steven Nadler

blackwell great minds

descartes

André Gombay

BLACKWELL PUBLISHING
350 Main Street, Malden, MA 02148-5020, USA
9600 Garsington Road, Oxford OX4 2DQ, UK
550 Swanston Street, Carlton, Victoria 3053, Australia

First published 2007 by Blackwell Publishing Ltd

1   2007

Library of Congress Cataloging-in-Publication Data

Gombay, André, 1933–
    Descartes / André Gombay.
      p. cm. — (Blackwell great minds)
    Includes bibliographical references and index.
    ISBN-13: 978-0-631-23345-9 (hardcover : alk. paper)
    ISBN-10: 0-631-23345-8 (hardcover : alk. paper)
    ISBN-13: 978-0-631-23346-6 (pbk. : alk. paper)
    ISBN-10: 0-631-23346-6 (pbk. : alk. paper)   1. Descartes, René, 1596–1650.   I.
Title.

    B1875.G559 2006
    194—dc22
                                                            2006020373

A catalogue record for this title is available from the British Library.

Set in 9.5/12pt Trump Mediaeval
by Graphicraft Limited, Hong Kong
Printed and bound in Singapore
by Markono Print Media Pte Ltd

The publisher's policy is to use permanent paper from mills that operate a sustainable
forestry policy, and which has been manufactured from pulp processed using acid-free
and elementary chlorine-free practices. Furthermore, the publisher ensures that the
text paper and cover board used have met acceptable environmental accreditation
standards.

For further information on
Blackwell Publishing, visit our website:
www.blackwellpublishing.com

To B.

contents

preface

May 2001: a Norwegian friend – no philosopher – has just written us a letter, a paean to the return of spring. She concludes: "How lucky I am: unlike Descartes I do not need to think in order to be!" The remark is plain, unsurprising, simply one more testimony to the fact that a certain dictum of Descartes' is the most famous sentence in philosophy, indeed one of the most famous sentences ever. In a curious way it resembles another monument of our culture, the *Mona Lisa*. It, too, has the smooth face and the secret smile, that portent of depths impossible to plumb. It, too, has a way of getting under one's skin, of eliciting reactions that go beyond intellectual or aesthetic appraisal. Dictum and painting alike arouse an urge to put down, or denigrate, or deface, or parody. Our Norwegian friend rejoices at being free of a tiresome constraint; viewers of the *Mona Lisa* will say "so what?" or shoot a bullet through the canvas. Have we not all seen Mona Lisa made up as a hag? or mustachioed? or winking? Don't we constantly come across parodies of the Cartesian sentence? "I run, therefore I am"? or (for academics) "I write, therefore I am"? or (one up) "I am read, therefore I am"? And countless more?

Nor is it just those five words of Descartes – the *cogito*, they are commonly called – that elicit these reactions: I am almost tempted to say that it is Descartes himself; and Descartes not just when he is read by philosophers. Some years ago after surgery for cancer, my wife decided not to heed the surgeon's advice to undergo chemotherapy as further treatment, and perhaps even radiation; but opted instead for a regimen that put the accent on relaxation, self-awareness and meditation – an approach to health that is commonly called *holistic*. Well, thanks to my wife's decision I soon learnt of another common idiom: in the circles in which she now moved, the standard way of referring to the medical approach that she had foresworn was to call it *Cartesian* medicine.

Another "unlike Descartes," then: perhaps "unlike Descartes, I do need to think in order to be healthy." And strangely, this new distancing fits in well with the earlier one – almost the reverse side of the coin, one might say. If you hold (Norwegianly) that there is more to you than mere thinking, you might also hold (holistic-therapeutically) that there is more to your body than mere ticking. You might reason like this. "Sheer thought isn't all that makes me what I am; other things are involved – feelings for example. And surely *they* are much entwined with what goes on in my body. So my body cannot be something that I own simply the way I own my car; and by the same token, preventing cancer from spreading in my body cannot be like preventing rust from spreading in my car. Yet that is exactly what Descartes (and my surgeon) would think."

Would they? or would Descartes? As we shall see, it is by no means a straight matter to tag him with this belief. Yes, he did say things in that vein: for example, he compared his body to a clock; but he said other things too, different – like telling Princess Elisabeth that she would not be rid of her fevers until she "made her soul happy."[1] It is interesting that he should nonetheless be singled out by public opinion as a hard-liner, and singled out so categorically. Nor do such imputations end here – let me mention one or two more, continuing to confine myself to episodes of my own life. A few months ago, on hearing that I was at work on the present book, my neighbor Clive sneered: "Ah! the man who said it was all right to beat one's dog." Again, not a new label. A 1650s visitor to Port-Royal School reports on how the children there enjoyed dissect-ing dogs that they had nailed live to wooden planks: after all, "their cries when hammered were nothing but the noises of some small springs that were being deranged"[2] – Descartes *dixit*. For its part, the *Encyclopedia Britannica* of 1801 devotes most of its entry on "brutes" to explaining why Descartes held that animals were automata, or *robots* as we might now say. One main reason, the writer tells us, is that this answered one great objection to God's goodness: that he should "suffer creatures who have never sinned to be subjected to so many miseries."[3]

As it happens, I have *not* come across that thought in Descartes, though he certainly did say that animals were automata. Yet he also sometimes spoke – seemingly without qualms – of animals expressing joy or hope.[4] So again we might ask: why was the brutal view at once so commonly ascribed to him?

The tags hung around Descartes' neck testify, I think, to two things. First, a certain quality of his prose; we shall have ample occasion to note it as we look at the texts. Descartes dislikes technical jargon; his sentences – their syntax, their vocabulary – are readily graspable as you read them; they feel fluid and plain. Think only of the *cogito*. Yet there is also a strange tinge to that plainness – the suggestion of a deeper hinter-land, a vista of things unsaid. Many readers have sensed this, and many have held it against him. Descartes is a philosopher who is often accused of being intellectually dishonest: he did not say all that he ought to have said. "Why did he *not* say outright that animals had no feelings, if he thought they were mere machines?" Or: "Why did he *not* say that stopping cancer was like stopping rust, if he thought human bodies were just complicated clocks?" So the charges go.

Still, it is not just a matter of prose quality: there is another, deeper, reason for the tags. Descartes is not the father of modern philosophy for nothing. All these views that are commonly assigned to him are ones that for the past three or four centuries have had a vivid life of their own: many of us – and not just philosophers – are preoccupied with them. We are attracted even when we disagree. To use a Freudian word, let us say that we are *ambivalent* and want someone to have spoken out these thoughts, if only perhaps then to distance ourselves from the speaker. "Unlike Descartes . . . ," we intone. What is more, that ambivalence sometimes extends to matters that did not interest anyone much when Descartes wrote of them, but have come to interest us now, and where again he is someone to whom we can ascribe a hard line. He did write – didn't he? – that "we cannot have a thought of which we are not conscious the very moment that it is in us."[5] Does this mean, then, that there can be no such thing as an unconscious feeling, or unconscious memory, or unconscious desire? To put it mildly, these matters have been a subject of some curiosity in the past hundred years – and not just to theorists of the mind. And if we are looking for a hardliner on one side, who is a better candidate than Descartes?

He is *that*. But then again, he is a philosopher who worried greatly about the fact that other people could know about him what he could not know himself – for example, the mistakes he was making; and who, in order to account for that imbalance, offered an engrossing analysis of the mental make-up in human beings that made making mistakes possible at all. In the same vein, when writing about feelings and emotions (he devoted an entire book to them), he takes pains to remind his readers that "those who are most strongly agitated by their passions are not the ones who know them best."[6] So once again, the portrait has more lines and shadows than appeared at first sight.

Let us look more intently, then – hoping that Mona Lisa's smile remains.

life and writings

M uch of what we know about Descartes' early life comes from a two-volume biography, *La Vie de Monsieur Descartes*, written by Adrien Baillet in 1691.

Born

(a) March 31, 1596, near Tours;

(b) into a family about to be ennobled; in fact, though apparently not wishing to be so addressed, Descartes is often called *Seigneur du Perron*;

(c) into a well-off family: he will have independent means, won't have to seek a patron.

School

(a) enters the *Collège de La Flèche* in 1606 or 1607, and stays for eight years;

(b) this was a Jesuit school founded in 1604; we know a lot about its curriculum of studies, thanks to the *Ratio studiorum* – a pedagogical treatise elaborated by the Jesuits in the 1580s and 1590s and strictly followed for the next two centuries in all their institutions; so that, for example, though born generations apart, Descartes and Molière and Voltaire would have had *exactly* the same school education; namely:

(c) five years of classical humanities, Latin and Greek; followed for those who stayed on by three years of "philosophy" – which meant a year of logic (Aristotelian), then a year of mathematics and Aristotelian physics, and finally a year of ethics (including casuistry), and metaphysics (basically Aristotelian);

(d) something else is important about Jesuit schooling: Jesuits are the first, in Europe, systematically to *mark* the work of schoolchildren – from good to bad, from best to worst. They mark by assigning letters or numbers; and mark not just the students' work, but the mental attitudes and aptitudes that the work evinces – like effort, assiduity, intelligence, interest, etc. Not only that, but now teachers also *rank* students according to the marks they have received. This happens in every subject and in every class. In fact teachers go even further, they have instituted signs of honor or dishonor according to the marks that students have achieved. They assign seats in the classroom according to rank; and at the end of the year there are celebrations where the school publicly honors the students ranked highest – "prize days," they are called. At the end of the year also, there are examinations to decide whether a student is to be promoted to the next higher class: dunces have to repeat their year.

University: 1615–16

Descartes studies law at Poitiers: the abstract of the dissertation for his law degree (on will-making), together with a dedication to his godfather, were found and published a dozen years ago. He will never practice.

Travels: 1616–29

Very little is known in detail or with certainty about this long stretch of Descartes' life. Here, however, are some more or less assured events:

1618 Beginning of the Thirty Years War: Descartes goes off to Holland, to join the army of Maurice of Nassau (Protestant).

1618–19 Spends winter in Breda, in southern Holland. Forges an intense friendship with a young Dutchman, Isaac Beeckman, with whom he discusses scientific issues. Descartes gives Beeckman as a personal present a treatise he has just written, the *Compendium Musicæ*; incidentally, Descartes is one of the few great philosophers – some others are Plato, Nietzsche, Wittgenstein – to have been keenly interested in music. As we shall see, music also has to do with the last piece he wrote, a few weeks before his death.

1619–20 Leaves Holland for southern Germany to join the army of Maximilian of Bavaria (Catholic); perhaps stays till the end of 1620; perhaps participates in the siege of Prague, and in the removal of Frederick from the throne of Bohemia.

November 10, 1619 On that day – St Martin's Eve – Descartes discovers "the foundations of a wonderful science," and in the night that follows has three vivid dreams which he describes in detail: did he regard them as omens of his life to come? We have that description via Baillet – who then, however, almost expunged it from the next edition of *La Vie*, doubtless to allay the thought that an oneiric experience lay at the birth of rationalist philosophy.

1620–5 We know very little about these years. Descartes travels widely, with occasional returns to France; befriends Marin Mersenne on one of them; goes to Italy, in particular on a pilgrimage to Loreto to fulfill a vow he had made on the night of the dreams; perhaps meets Claudio Monteverdi in Venice in 1624.

1625–7 Descartes is in Paris – his only long sojourn there. Meets everyone who is anyone in the world of intellect, *chez* Mersenne and elsewhere: mathematicians (Hardy, Morin, Debeaune); writers (Guez de Balzac); theologians – mostly Oratorian rigorists (Bérulle, Gibieuf). Two events are perhaps noteworthy (Baillet places them in November 1628, but they probably occurred about a year earlier):

(a) The Chandoux lecture. Before an assembly of bright minds at the Papal Nuncio's palace, a Parisian wit named Chandoux gave a talk where he attacked Aristotelian philosophy; everyone applauded – except Descartes. Pressed to explain, Descartes promptly showed how harmless the assault had been: with such enemies, did Aristotle need any friends?

(b) Meeting with Bérulle, a few days after the Chandoux episode. Bérulle, who had been present, summoned Descartes to an interview, where he told him that he (Descartes) owed it to God to give the world a new philosophy. Descartes left Paris soon afterward.

Holland: 1629–49

In the spring of 1629 Descartes goes to Holland, where he will stay for the next 20 years except for a few brief trips abroad, including three returns to France, in 1644, 1647, and 1648. We know much more about this portion of his life. For one thing, as he becomes famous, accounts by others begin to appear. Second and more important, still extant is a large correspondence – letters to and from him. They are of course mostly about philosophy or science, but not entirely. On occasion, they reveal quite a bit about Descartes, or about his correspondent.

Here are a few dates: my division into periods is quite arbitrary.

1629–37 Descartes' interests are mostly scientific: he mentions in 1629 that he has begun a short treatise on metaphysics, but apparently does not pursue the project. He corresponds about astronomy, optics, the laws of motion, the circulation of the blood, geometry, and algebra. He does not publish anything till 1637.

Autumn 1629 First letter to Mersenne – the beginning of a long correspondence. Mersenne is foremost remembered today as Descartes' correspondent and intellectual agent; but in his lifetime he was known in his own right as a philosopher, scientist, musical theorist, prolific writer of vast volumes, and, perhaps most important, as an intellectual middleman. He wrote thousands of letters, corresponded with many thinkers and scientists – Galileo, Grotius, Fermat, Torricelli, Pascal – fostering interchange and discussion. We know of more than 300 letters between Descartes and Mersenne, of which about one half is extant – almost all from the philosopher's pen: Descartes seems not to have thought Mersenne's missives worth keeping.

Spring 1632 Meets Constantijn Huygens. Huygens was secretary to Maurice of Nassau – a demanding and influential post – but he was also a Renaissance man, keenly interested in science and the arts. He and Descartes see each other quite often and exchange many letters, though not many about philosophical subjects: after Mersenne, Huygens is Descartes' most frequent correspondent.

November 1633 Hearing of the Inquisition's condemnation of Galileo, Descartes decides not to publish – indeed not to finish – *Le Monde*, where he, too, defended a version of Copernicanism; he also leaves unfinished *L'Homme*, a treatise meant to accompany *Le Monde*.

June 1635 Birth of Francine, daughter of Descartes and Helena Jans, his housekeeper.

June 1637 Publication in Leiden, and without Descartes' name, of the *Discours de la méthode*, followed by three *Essais* presented as illustrations of that method: *La Dioptrique*, *Les Météores*, and *La Géométrie*.

1637–42 These are the central years in the elaboration of Descartes' metaphysics.

1637 Cartesianism has its first airing in academe: Descartes' doctrines are taught at the University of Utrecht by Reneri and by Regius.

September 1640 Francine dies. Descartes alludes to her death in a letter of January 1641, writing that he is "not one of those who think that tears and sadness belong only to women."

1641 (Paris) and 1642 (Amsterdam) Publication of the *Meditationes de prima philosophia*, followed by six (Paris), eventually seven (Amsterdam), sets of *Objectiones* and *Responsiones*.

1642–9 New enemies, new friends.

1642 Beginning of Descartes' difficulties with Dutch universities. At Utrecht he is accused by the rector Voetius of various religious or theological sins: atheism, pelagianism (the view that human beings can avoid sin even without God's grace), and other heresies. Charges and countercharges fly for years; at one point in 1643, Descartes even fears arrest, and appeals to the French ambassador for protection.

1642 or 1643 Descartes meets Princess Elisabeth of Bohemia, oldest daughter of Frederick, whom Descartes (perhaps) helped depose from his Prague throne in 1620: the family has lived in exile in The Hague ever since. Elisabeth and Descartes are to become friends. They see each other, they correspond – there are about 60 letters extant, many written during a period of intense intellectual interchange between 1644 and 1646. Elisabeth's views and interests are almost certainly what prompted Descartes to reflect on feelings and emotions, and led him eventually to write the *Passions de l'âme*.

June 1644 Descartes' first trip back to France in 15 years; while there, he meets and befriends Hector-Pierre Chanut, a slightly younger Jesuit school alumnus and now about to become French attaché to Sweden (this was an important post: remember, France and Sweden were the two main powers on one side of the Thirty Years War).

Summer 1644 Publication in Amsterdam of the *Principia Philosophiæ*: the book is dedicated to Elisabeth.

November 1644 Descartes returns to Holland.

Spring 1646 Descartes gives Elisabeth a manuscript on human feelings – a *traité des passions*, he calls it.

August 1646 Elisabeth must leave Holland because of a family scandal. She goes off to Germany, taking Descartes' manuscript with her. Elisabeth hoped her exile would last only half a year; but she was never to return, never to see Descartes again.

Winter 1646–7 Difficulties begin with the University of Leiden: Descartes is accused by theologians there – again of atheism, again of heresy.

January 1647 Descartes receives a letter from Chanut, conveying questions from Queen Christina – about love. He replies on February 1; and to further questions from the Queen on that subject, in a further letter on June 6, where he confesses to having as a child fallen in love with a cross-eyed young girl and having as a result been attracted to cross-eyed women for many years afterwards.

Summer 1647 Descartes goes to France again, even considers staying there – a reaction to the problems with Utrecht and Leiden. However, he returns to Holland in November. During his stay in France, he meets young Blaise Pascal and encourages him to make experiments about atmospheric pressure.

November 1647 Descartes sends to Christina through Chanut a copy of the draft of the *traité des passions*, plus copies of some of his letters to Elisabeth on passions and the good life.

1648 The treaties of Westphalia are signed, bringing to an end the Thirty Years War: France and Sweden are the victors.

Sweden: 1649–50

March 1649 Descartes receives an invitation from Christina to come to Sweden. With some reluctance he accepts; he will leave Holland at the end of August and arrive in Stockholm early in October.

Autumn–winter 1649 Descartes' visit is hardly a success: the Queen has too many interests beside philosophy.

November 1649 Publication in Paris and in Amsterdam of the *Passions de l'âme* – an expanded version of the *traité* Descartes had first sent to Elisabeth in 1646.

December 1649 Descartes (perhaps?) writes the verse for a ballet called *La Naissance de la paix*, which celebrates Christina's 23rd birthday and the advent of peace after a long murderous war.

February 11, 1650 Descartes dies in Stockholm, of pneumonia.

If the fate of philosophers is to be "exiles in their own land," then Descartes must surely count as the quintessential philosopher – except that his exile was not figurative but real, not forced but freely chosen, not temporary but permanent. From the age of 22 he spent almost no time in France. Why? The simplest and most likely answer is that he yearned for aloofness and anonymity – many events in his life testify to this. For example, urging a fellow Frenchman to come and live in Amsterdam, he writes: "in this large city, everyone but myself is engaged in trade and hence so attentive to his own profit that I could live here all my life without being seen by a soul". This is praise. Some years later he tells Mersenne of having gone to hear a well-known Calvinist preacher, "but in such a manner that anyone seeing me would know I wasn't there as a believer. For I came in only as the sermon began, stood by the door and, the moment it was finished, went out without staying for the rituals." Delight at not being seen, arriving late, standing by the door, walking out early: these are deep traits of Descartes' personality. This is not to say he had no close friends – Constantijn Huygens, Elisabeth, Pierre Chanut are proof to the contrary. Still, here is the motto which in October 1646 he told Chanut he had adopted from Seneca:

A sad death awaits him
Who, too well known to all,
Dies unknown to himself.

Writings

Works published during Descartes' lifetime

As we have seen, there are four main works – two in Latin and two in French:

I. 1637. *Discours de la méthode*, followed by three *Essais*: *La Dioptrique*, *Les Météores*, and *La Géométrie*.

II.   1641–2. *Meditationes de prima philosophia*, followed by *Objectiones cum responsionibus authoris*.
III.   1644. *Principia Philosophiæ*.
IV.   1649. *Passions de l'âme*.

I. *Discours* and *Essais*

The section that has most interested philosophers is of course the introduction to the *Essais*, namely the *Discours de la méthode* (in English, *Discourse on Method*). It is now a classic – partly because of its urbane, flowing, and utterly untechnical style.

The *Discourse* is a short intellectual autobiography, in six untitled parts. It first tells the reader about Descartes' schooldays; then (Part 2) about thoughts he has had on the right method for finding truth in science – always seek certainty; then (Part 3) about the rules he has seen fit to adopt in everyday conduct, where certainty is impossible: Descartes calls them a "provisional ethic" (*morale par provision*). The fourth Part retails thoughts he has had on metaphysics: here is where the dictum "*je pense, donc je suis*" appears for the first time. Part 5 tells, among other things, how Descartes came to think that animals were plain machines, or *automata*. (Incidentally, that is about the only published text where Descartes states and argues for that view – it became at once one of his best-known and most controversial doctrines.) Part 6 is largely concerned with reminiscences about engaging in scientific work: one lesson Descartes says he has learnt is that one is better off relying on paid underlings than working with colleagues of one's own rank – *these* can never be trusted to do what they have promised.

The three *Essais* are now mostly of historical interest. *La Dioptrique* (*Dioptrics*, or sometimes *Optics*) is about the nature of light, lenses, and sight. *Les Météores* (*Meteors*) is about weather: wind, clouds, rain, snow, lightning, rainbows. *La Géométrie* deals with the interplay between geometric curves and algebraic formulae – it is one of the pioneer works of analytic geometry.

A Latin translation of the *Discours* and the first two *Essais*, approved and overseen by Descartes, came out in 1644 as the *Specimina Philosophiæ*.

II. *Meditationes de prima philosophia* and *Objectiones cum responsionibus authoris* (*Meditations on First Philosophy* and *Objections and Replies*)

The *Meditations* are basically an elaboration of Part 4 of the *Discourse*. In 1640, and with Descartes' approval, Mersenne sent the short manuscript (about 85 pages) to various philosophers and theologians, asking for comments; so that, when the *Meditations* came out the following year in Paris, the volume also featured six sets of *Objections*, each set followed by Descartes' *Replies* – 450 pages in all. The objectors are in two instances unnamed (*Second* and *Sixth* set): they are widely supposed to be Mersenne himself, and perhaps friends of his. Otherwise, they are (in order): Caterus, a Dutch clergyman; Hobbes, the English philosopher then living in exile in Paris; Arnauld, a young French theologian soon to befriend Pascal; and the French philosopher Gassendi.

The 1642 Amsterdam edition contains two further texts: a *Seventh* set of *Objections*, from the Jesuit father Bourdin, followed as usual by Descartes' *Replies*; and then the so-titled *Letter to Dinet*. Descartes – taking Bourdin to have been commissioned by the Jesuits to voice their reaction to the *Meditations* – writes publicly to Dinet, the head of the French province of the Order, to protest against the choice of spokesman: he thinks Bourdin for the most part ill-intentioned and obtuse. Incidentally, the *Letter* features what is probably Descartes' boldest anti-Aristotelian statement: "there isn't a single answer given according to the principles of peripatetic philosophy that I cannot demonstrate to be invalid and false." He is usually more circumspect.

A French translation of the *Meditations* and of the *Objections and Replies* came out in 1647, approved by Descartes – up to a point. In accordance with Descartes' wishes, Bourdin's *Objections* were excised from the translation. But against his wishes, Gassendi's *Objections* were retained, though their message was further diminished by a short letter Descartes appended to his *Reply*, where he answers – very condescendingly – queries summarized from the *Disquisitio Metaphysica*, a large tome that Gassendi had composed in reply to Descartes' *Replies* to his own *Objections*.

III. The *Principia Philosophiæ* (*Principles of Philosophy*)

In a sense this is Descartes' *magnum opus*. It consists of about 500 numbered articles, grouped into four parts. Part 1 is metaphysics – a summary of the *Meditations*; Parts 2, 3, and 4 are Descartes' vision of the material universe, and include doctrines that he had held back from publishing ten years earlier, when he heard of Galileo's condemnation. They concern space, matter, the laws of motion; gravity; solids and liquids, fire, magnetism; stars and the solar system, etc. etc. Toward the end of Part 4 (art. 188), Descartes tells the reader that he had planned to write two further parts, one on animals and plants, the other on human beings – but had lacked time to carry out the experiments that were needed.

A French translation came out in 1647, approved and overseen by Descartes. It included a new preface, with the famous image comparing knowledge to a tree whose "roots are metaphysics; trunk, physics; and the branches that stem from the trunk, all the other sciences – which can be reduced to three main ones: medicine, mechanics and morals."

Descartes hoped that the *Principia* would be adopted as a textbook in Jesuit colleges. They were not. In fact, Descartes' entire work was put on the Index of the Catholic Church soon after his death.

IV. The *Passions de l'âme* (*Passions of the Soul*)

This appeared in the autumn of 1649, after Descartes had left for Sweden – it is not clear that he ever saw the published book. Like the *Principles* it is written in numbered paragraphs – more than 200 of them. Descartes declares in the preface that he intends to explain passions solely "*en physicien*" ("as a physicist"); but he in fact often discusses them from a moral standpoint, especially in the third and final part.

Three other works of Descartes came out during his life:

1643   *Epistola ad G. Voetium*;
1645   *Lettre apologétique*;
1647   *Notæ in programma quoddam*.

These are all polemical, having to do with Descartes' problems with Utrecht. The first is an answer to his enemy Voetius; the second, a complaint to the Utrecht City Council about how he has been treated; in the third (*Comments on a Certain Broadsheet*), Descartes distances himself from his former Utrecht disciple now disowned, Regius.

Works published after Descartes' death

Five are volume-length but unfinished:

L'Homme (*Treatise on Man*) and *Le Monde* (*World*). These are the treatises Descartes decided to abandon writing in 1633 when he heard of Galileo's condemnation.
Regulæ ad directionem ingenii (*Rules for the Direction of the Mind*). This piece is something of a mystery, never mentioned by Descartes but found in a chest of manuscripts that he had taken to Sweden. The *Regulæ* are presumed to be an early work, perhaps written in the 1620s – about how to reason properly.
La Recherche de la vérité par la lumière naturelle (*The Search for Truth by the Natural Light*). Again never mentioned by Descartes, again found in the chest. This is an unfinished dialogue, on subjects closely

resembling the early *Meditations*, therefore presumed to have been written roughly when they were, in the early 1640s.

La Description du corps humain (*The Description of the Human Body*), sometimes called *De la formation du fœtus* (*On the Formation of the Fetus*). This was written in the late 1640s, perhaps to make up that Part 6 of the *Principles* – on human beings – that Descartes reported in 1644, in Part 4 of the book, not to have had time to compose. The *Description* is unfinished.

Other fragments have come down to us, on mathematics, embryology, anatomy, even metaphysics – again found in the chest in Stockholm. They range from a notebook dating back to Descartes' first journey to Holland and Germany (the so-called *Cogitationes Privatæ* (*Private Thoughts*)), to much later texts like the *De Generatione animalium* (*On the Generation of Animals*).

To this list we should add three titles – two of them with a question mark:

1 The *Compendium Musicæ*: as we saw, Descartes' first work – a 1619 present to his friend Beeckman but not published till after his death.
2 *La Naissance de la paix* (?): as we saw, Descartes' last work (if indeed by him) – the verse for a ballet performed at Queen Christina's birthday in December 1649; it was published in 1920.
3 The so-called *Conversation* with Burman (?): in April 1648, Descartes was interviewed over lunch by a young Dutchman, Frans Burman, and asked questions about his philosophy. The next day Burman transcribed the answers – we now have that text. On the other hand, Descartes himself almost certainly never saw it: whether it is an authoritative statement of his thoughts depends on the accuracy of the transcription.

Correspondence

Extant today are about 530 letters, of which about 400 are from Descartes' pen and 130 from correspondents. It should be added that this count is somewhat arbitrary – it being sometimes a matter of editorial decision what to count as separate letters; a matter of editorial decision, too, how to affix a date or a correspondent. A further 60 letters are mentioned or described by Baillet, but their text has not come down to us.

This is a big corpus, then – in fact larger than all the other Cartesian writings put together. The table opposite shows some numbers (letters from Descartes are on the left of the hyphen; letters to him, on the right).[1]

Beeckman (1619–34)	8
Mersenne (1629–48)	130–50
Huygens and brother-in-law Wilhem (1632–49)	90–40
Regius (1640–5)	18–3
Elisabeth and her sister Sophie (1643–9)	36–26
Chanut and Christina (1646–9)	14–4
Jesuits (1637–46)	27–6
English philosophers (Hobbes, Morus) (1641–9)	5–6

As we shall see, some of Descartes' most striking doctrines are expounded there rather than in the published work.

Current editions of Descartes

The most complete is *Œuvres de Descartes*, ed. Charles Adam and Paul Tannery (rev. edn. Paris: Vrin/CNRS, 1964–76).

It has 11 volumes, two of which (8 and 9) are further divided into subvolumes *a* and *b*. This is now the standard edition, and likely to remain so for a long time. In fact, recently published volumes of Descartes' work – in any language – almost invariably carry in the margin the volume- and page-numbers of the corresponding Adam and Tannery text; likewise for references to Descartes in writings about him. The lines that I quoted above, about not being seen by a soul in Amsterdam, would be referenced like this: *letter* to Balzac, May 5, 1631 (AT 1, 203); and the passage about the tree of knowledge, like this: *Principles*, Preface to the French edition (AT 9b, 14). I shall follow that practice.

The most extensive English edition is *The Philosophical Writings of Descartes*, translated by John Cottingham, Robert Stoothoff, and Dugald Murdoch (Cambridge: Cambridge University Press, 1985–91).

This has three volumes, of which the third is devoted to the correspondence and involves a further translator, Anthony Kenny. Current English-language literature on Descartes often also locates texts with reference to that edition. So the letter to Balzac would carry the further indication: CSMK, 31; and the tree-of-knowledge passage, CSM 1, 186. I shall also follow that practice, even when my translation diverges from CSM or CSMK.

There is also a CD-ROM edition: *Œuvres complètes de René Descartes* (Connaught Project-University of Toronto, Charlottesville, Intelex, 2001).

distrust and deception

I n a letter of June 1643 (AT 3, 692–3; CSMK, 227) Descartes tells Princess Elisabeth that, as a rule, he spends only a few hours a year thinking about metaphysics, while he devotes some hours each day to thoughts on mathematics and on the shapes and motions of bodies. We should certainly take the letter seriously: the greater part of Descartes' opus is indeed scientifically oriented. Think only of the *Essays*, of the bulk of the *Principles*, of the various unfinished works, for example on embryology. It happens that, in its detail, Cartesian science is now merely of historic interest – say, the pronouncement in article 65 of Part 4 of the *Principles* (AT 8a, 245) that water flows on earth as blood does in our body, in a circle from mountains down to the sea in what we call "rivers," and then back to the mountains again, in subterranean ducts. So be it. But the same in no way holds true of the general principles to which Descartes appealed as he worked at his science, for example the tenet that there is no structural difference between clocks and natural bodies (*Principles*, Part 4, art. 203: AT 8a, 326; CSM 1, 288) – the difference between a live and a dead body amounting to no more than the difference between a working and a broken clock (*Passions*, art. 6: AT 11, 330–1; CSM 1, 329–30). Is there nothing special, then, about organic life? Or take the injunction of the *Principles* (Part 3, art. 2: AT 8a, 80–1; CSM 1, 248) that we should never ask of a natural thing what it is *for*: for such an inquiry would presume that we can discover God's purposes, an impossible task. Does this mean, then, that it is unscientific and presumptuous of me to wonder what the function of my liver is? These are matters that posterity has continued to debate, to this day.[1]

I shall, however, not debate them in this book; but will focus my attention on the thoughts that preoccupied Descartes only a few hours a year. In the Cartesian opus I shall confine myself to two works: the *Meditations* – they are what made Descartes "the father of modern philosophy"[2] – and the *Passions of the Soul*, because there too he stands at a turn of European thought, perhaps not as the lone guiding star, but as a member of a bright constellation. Also, looking at the *Passions* will correct an over-intellectualized image of Descartes that we have inherited.

To the *Meditations*, then – with some trepidation. After all, they are the most read, most translated, most written-about book in modern western philosophy. When they first appeared, it was, as we saw, with an appendage of objections penned by other philosophers, three times the length of the work itself. Well, the flow hasn't stopped: analyses, exegeses, commentaries, refutations – a seemingly endless tide of thoughts, words, and paper. To count just translations, for example, at least six have come out in English in the last 50 years: not exactly a drought.

Descartes would have savored the attention, of course, and not merely because it was flattering; more important, he would have regarded it as confirming the aptness of the idiom he had chosen for conveying his thoughts. Even at first glance, the *Meditations* will strike you as extraordinary. Here is a book written in the first person, but not an autobiography as the *Discourse on Method* had been. No, the text is in the present tense: these are thoughts unfolding right now. And they will continue to unfold for six days, as many days as there are *Meditation*s – that fiction being more or less sustained throughout. What is more, inside a *Meditation* there are no paragraphs, the text goes on without a break.[3] The whole work is without a footnote, without a single mention of any philosopher, or anyone else for that matter.[4] In the entire piece there is basically just one proper noun: *God*.

Commentators have not been slow in perceiving a religious aura about the book. There is that noun, of course – repeated 80 times; and also a more general fact, a lineage. From his schooldays, Descartes would have been acquainted with a tradition of Christian religious writing called, as it happens, "meditation." Works in that lineage had two standard features: they were written in the first person – the reader being, so to speak (and I speak Freudianly here), asked to *identify* with the writer; and they were *ascentional* – the meditator, as he or she went on, getting ever closer to the Truth. The first objective is stressed by Descartes even before he begins: "I would not urge anyone to read this book except those who are able and willing to meditate seriously with me," says the *Preface to the reader* (AT 7, 9; CSM 2, 8). This is not a mere figure of style, but should be taken literally: it accounts, for example, for the bare non-technical aspect of the book. There is no need of footnotes – Descartes is not writing for scholars, not seeking to situate himself with respect to past thinkers in the field. Nor is he speaking from on high – this is not a master addressing pupils: what is sought is a relationship where reader and writer become mentally one. Incidentally, the notion of *making oneself one* with someone or something will (as we shall see) play a key role at an important moment of Descartes' progress, so the thought voiced in the *Preface* would come naturally enough to him. And of course that thought is attractive anyhow – don't we want teachers to be on a level with us? But sadly, there is also a downside to this approach, at least as Descartes uses it. As we know, he was faced with questions and objections: Mersenne had solicited them on his behalf. Well, more often than not Descartes is abusive as he replies; he regards his objector as willfully inattentive or ill-intentioned – he has not really tried to meditate with him. For example, he never addresses Hobbes by name, only refers to him as "the Englishman"; Gassendi, he calls "oh, flesh"; Bourdin, he thinks obtuse and wants erased from the French edition. The tone is of course different when he answers queens or princesses, but overall one gets the definite impression that Descartes does not regard philosophy as a subject where genuine and honest differences of opinion may occur. Spiritual intimacy has its costs.

The second standard feature of traditional meditation, the ascentional character, is also clearly discernible in our text. It is as though Descartes were climbing a mountain – not straight up but obliquely, circling in a spiral so that the old landscapes keep reappearing, each time seen from higher up. Even the titles of the individual *Meditations* bear witness to this. *What can be called in doubt*, says the First; *On truth and falsity*, will say the Fourth. Likewise, *Of the nature of the human mind; that it is better known than the body* (Second) will be echoed by *Of the existence of material things and of the real distinction between mind and body* (Sixth); and *Of God, that he exists* (Third) heralds *Of the essence of material things; and of God again, that he exists* (Fifth). The spiraling, too, is apt to create problems. Things viewed early in the climb may well appear different – perhaps clearer – from a higher vantage point: so as we see them again, should we (the readers) simply disregard the vision we had three days ago? or rather say that we didn't have a full sight then? And there are even deeper headaches. Is it plain that the view from the higher coil will always be clearer than it was lower down? Could it not in fact have become the opposite, blurred by the height or the rarefied air? Nor is this a worry I raise in the abstract: in one specific case and hardly a minor one – the division of mind and body – the philosopher whom posterity has remembered is much more the Descartes of *Meditation Two* than the Descartes supposedly at the apex of the climb, in *Meditation Six*. This is a tricky question, which we shall have to face in due course.

But enough of allusions and generalities: it is time to look at the text. To *Meditation One*, then.

It begins sternly enough. Descartes remembers how often he has mistaken the false for the true, and, to avoid recurrence of that misfortune, he resolves to devote himself to the overthrow of his own convictions. How to do that? He hits at once (AT 7, 18; CSM 2, 12) on the precept to follow:

never trust fully those who have deceived you even once.

Commonsensical enough – yet Descartes' readers should certainly give the adage a closer look, even at first encounter. For though it will, strictly speaking, serve Descartes only for the first steps on the road, thoughts central to it will govern not just *Meditation One* but everything that follows, till the very last page. Let us reflect a bit, then, on the two key words – *trust* and *deceive*.

Remember the fable of the little boy who cried "wolf!" He was believed once, believed maybe twice – and then came to a doleful end. Ask yourself why the story is recounted at all: clearly, it is to warn against telling fibs or lies. If you engage in untruths (and are discovered!), you will forswear people's confidence, you will lose their trust, and sooner or later pay the price. Let me now add a twist to the story. Suppose that in the boy's village there stands a church with a clock-tower, whose clock tells the time with great accuracy – up to a point. The hands on the dial rotate with absolute punctuality; but when the wheel that activates the ringing of the hours is rewound (as it needs to be every day) the rewinding is apt to desynchronize the chime – the bell will ring four times, say, at three o'clock. This does not happen at every rewinding, but it happens; and the village lacks the funds to have the wheel set right.

In the fable, the villagers lost trust in the boy's cries; odds are that in my expanded tale they will also have lost trust in the chime of the clock. Two losses, then; yet how different. Gone in one case is confidence in a person's truthfulness; gone in the other, confidence in a contraption's reliability. The little boy wished to fool his elders; clocks wish nothing. Go back now to Descartes' adage "never trust . . ." and ask yourself: is the adage about trust in honesty, or trust in reliability? about trusting people, or trusting things?[5] Given that in the text the object of the verb *confidere* ("trust") is *illis qui* ("those who"), it must be about people; but Descartes will at once cross the line and apply the dictum to a non-person – his sense of sight, when he looks at things far or small. The crossover is made all the easier by the fact that the other verb in the dictum also has that ambivalence. Just as the idiom of trust occurs naturally in what appear at first sight to be two distinct contexts – sincerity and reliability – so the idiom of deception straddles the line between personal and impersonal. It would be perfectly appropriate to say that the chime of the village clock was deceptive, just as it was appropriate earlier to say that the boy's cries were deceptive. In one case (the cries), it was deception in a strong sense, meaning: intention to foster false belief. There is no like intention in the clock, only the likelihood that false belief may be fostered by it. Note that we seem to pass without chasm or zeugma from the chime to the cries: in both instances we speak of deceptiveness in what seems to be the same tone of voice. In fact, in Latin the problem is almost the other way around: how to separate the two. For *falli* – the standard Latin verb, which Descartes standardly uses – is either the deponent, meaning "err" or "go wrong," or the straight passive of *fallere*, where the active means "deceive" or "make go wrong". So it is often left to the reader to decide whether Descartes is talking about being mistaken, or being taken in.

One final (preliminary) remark on the intercourse of dishonesty and unreliability. Go back to the villagers' clock: could it not also be deceptive in what I have called the stronger sense? Could it not be *rigged* – its chime having been deliberately so made as to mislead, say, newcomers or the sightless? In fact, there is almost an organic link between machinery (let me call the clock a "machine") and aptness for that kind of occurrence. Think only of words like *machination, craft, fabrication, make-up, artifice*: is it mere happenstance that they entwine instrument-making with trickery? We shall have ample occasion to ponder this marriage as we follow the *Meditations*.

For the moment, though, we are only at the first step – Descartes' remembering that he has been deceived by his eyes about things small or distant. He doesn't cite instances, but elsewhere (*Dioptrics*: AT 6, 147; CSM 1, 175; or *Meditation Six*: AT 7, 76; CSM 2, 53) he gives the example of square towers: they look round when viewed from afar. Well, imagine that you are approaching the boy's village, a first-time visitor, and while still at a distance you discern the church tower. Of course it looks round. But mindful of past vicissitudes, you follow Descartes' precept, you do not trust your eyes, you do not yet believe that the tower is round – you *doubt* that it is round.

We have just met the canonical word. It occurs in the opening sentence of the *Meditations* ("doubtful edifice"); it will occur two sentences from their close ("I ought not to have the slightest doubt") and dozens of times in between. It is the word (*dubium* as a noun, *dubitare* as a verb) that Descartes uses to designate the mental stance he has introduced through the notion of not-trusting – a stance to which posterity will give a special name: it will call it "Cartesian doubt." One might well ask, why the honor? There does not seem to be anything particularly special in the mental state of doubting what your eyes tell you about the tower. The psychology of it seems plain enough: you don't believe that the tower is round; you don't believe that it isn't round; you hold off believing anything in the matter. A pretty humdrum experience, it would seem – why glorify (or vilify?) it with a philosopher's name?

True enough – so far. We should not forget, however, that, as is usual with Descartes, the slope is about to get steeper. The policy of withholding belief will soon become harder to follow, and call for strategies that go well beyond the adage of distrust with which Descartes began. Take the next (AT 7, 19; CSM 2, 13) instance he records of his having been deluded (*delusus*):

> how often, asleep at night, am I convinced that I am here in my dressing-gown, sitting by the fire, when I am in fact lying without any clothes, between sheets!

In one sense, yes, this falls under the adage: dreams have deceived Descartes about his present posture and place, just as his eyes have deceived him about the shape of distant towers. Yet even a moment's reflection will disclose how different the new situation is – how much more complicated, psychologically. The earlier doubt might have been voiced like this: "It looks to me as though the tower is round; but I am far away; so perhaps the tower is not round." Well, let us formulate the dream-doubt in parallel fashion: "It looks to me as though I am seated by the fire; but I am dreaming; so perhaps I am not seated by the fire." Something sounds askew here, even at first hearing. One oddity is the second clause. There do exist "lucid" dreams – dreams that one is aware of having and where, if one spoke, one might say "I am now dreaming that. . . ." In fact Descartes is reported by his biographer Baillet to have had precisely one such on that memorable night of the three dreams, on St Martin's Eve in 1619: "not only did he decide, while sleeping, that this was a dream, but he even interpreted it before sleep left him" (*La Vie de Monsieur Descartes*, vol. 1, p. 51; quoted in AT 10, 184). So be it; but lucid dreams are an anomaly, and surely we cannot require our Cartesian doubter to be having just that kind. So in the statement of his doubt we must weaken the second clause – say, by inserting a "perhaps". It will now go like this: "It looks to me as though I am seated by the fire; but perhaps I am dreaming; so perhaps I am not seated by the fire." That sounds better; but even thus rephrased, the statement leaves an important thing unsaid. Consider the first clause now: does it really fit the doubter's mind? Does it merely *look* to him as though he is sitting? isn't it rather that he is *certain* of this – we know perfectly well what our actual posture is. So must he not rather be taken to be saying: "I am sure of being seated by the fire; but perhaps I am dreaming; so perhaps I am not seated by the fire"? Nor is this last emendation a small matter; it points to an essential feature of Cartesian doubt. Increasingly, that doubt will ask the doubter to say "perhaps no" where he is naturally disposed to say "of course yes"; it will require him to set aside not mere impressions (as in the case of the tower), but downright certainties – all in the name of some supposition he is making about himself and his present state.

"Suppose then that I am dreaming and that these particulars – that my eyes are open, that I am moving my head and stretching out my hands – are not true. Perhaps, indeed, I do not even have such hands or such body at all" (AT 7, 19; CSM 2, 13). Take that last sentence seriously: the distrust-adage, combined with memory of how often his dreams have deceived him, will enable Descartes to dismiss as dubious entire bulks of beliefs that we in fact consider to be sciences – "physics, astronomy, medicine" (that is *his* list, a few lines after the sentence I have just quoted); and dismiss them not because they harbor the odd mistake, but for the much more radical reason that their very subject – say the human body, in the case of medicine – may not exist at all, or not be at all like what we take it to be. So this is a massive doubt.

Yet Descartes will not pursue it for more than a few moments – his reason being that it is not massive enough: it leaves too many convictions unturned. Dreams, he argues, may be likened to paintings. No matter how fictitious or fantastic the scene depicted on a canvas may be, some things in it cannot be fictitious – for example that here is a spot of blue. In that sense, painting takes the existence of color for granted. Well, the same holds for dreams. No matter how unreal the events experienced in them may be, some components must be real: for example time and place, as general characteristics. Otherwise there would be no events, not even dream-events. Likewise for shape, location, numbers – these must all be taken to be actual features of the world. So there are lots of beliefs that even the supposition that one is dreaming will not shake (AT 7, 20; CSM 2, 14).

It is difficult not to second-guess Descartes here. Earlier in the argument, the fact that he had been deceived by dreams about the posture of his body authorized the supposition that he might have no such body at all. Why should the fact (say) that he has often wrongly dreamt that 91 was a prime number not similarly authorize Descartes to suppose that there might be no such things as primes? Why the discrepancy between the extent of the doubt legitimated in one case and in the other? Why should the dream-doubt leave the certainty of numbers intact? It is difficult to resist the suspicion that Descartes sets this rather arbitrary-looking limit because, deep down, he is not interested in dreams.[6] On the last page of the *Meditations* he will casually announce that there is after all a test for wakefulness: "when I see distinctly where things come from . . . and can without a break connect my perception of them with the whole of the rest of my life, then I am quite certain that I am not asleep but awake" (AT 7, 90; CSM 2, 62). This is the so-called coherence test – an ancient medicine, whose efficacy still needs showing. Could I not simply be dreaming that my present perceptions cohere with my past life? Descartes leaves it at that.

There is nothing casual, on the other hand, in the next reason for doubt that he proffers.

> Firmly rooted in my mind is the long-standing opinion that there is an omnipotent God who made me the kind of creature I am. How do I know that he has not brought it about that there is no earth, no sky, no extended thing, no shape, no size, no place, while nonetheless all these things appear to me to exist just as they do now? What is more, since I judge that others go wrong where they think they have the most perfect knowledge, may I not similarly be mistaken every time I add two and three or count the sides of a square, or even in a simpler matter if that is imaginable? But perhaps God has not allowed me to be so deceived, since he is said to be supremely good. But if it were inconsistent with his goodness to have created me such that I am deceived all the time, it would seem equally foreign to his goodness to allow me to be deceived occasionally – which can certainly not be said (AT 7, 21; CSM 2, 14).

In one sentence: how do I know that God has not made me such that I am always mistaken?

Posterity has given this question a name; it calls it the "deceiving God hypothesis." The hypothesis stands of course at the centre of Cartesian doubt – but not just there. It will have a far broader reach in the *Meditations*: once evoked, the specter of the deceiving God never vanishes; it will deflect the argument at almost every turn, in the way in which a prism deflects the light that is beamed through it. We shall meet it many times; let me for the moment confine myself to some opening generalities.

The idea must have come to Descartes in the late 1630s, for there is no mention of the deceiving God in Part 4 of the *Discourse on Method*, the 1637 text that prefigures the *Meditations*. However, if we look around in the early seventeenth century, we find thoughts of God and of deceit entwined often enough. "As no man can deceive God, so God can deceive no man," John Donne tells the faithful in St Paul's Cathedral on Christmas Day 1625.[7] The same pairing occurs in the theological works of Francisco Suárez (1548–1617). Is it a mortal sin, when confessing to a priest, to accuse oneself of a mortal sin one has in fact *not* committed? asks the *Integrity of Confession* – yes. Could God ever wish to deceive human beings? – no, says the *Treatise on Faith*.[8] In 1625 (the year of Donne's sermon) the topic of God's deception is discussed in a legal tome, Hugo Grotius' *Rights of War and Peace*: "no matter how supreme God's right over human beings . . . lying is alien to him."[9] Grotius refers his readers back to book III of the *Republic*, where Plato berates the poets for crediting Zeus with disguises. What need has God of subterfuge? To cover up ignorance? – he knows all; to hide the truth from a mad friend? – no friend of God is a madman; to subdue enemies? – he fears none (382d–e).

So the nexus between God and deceit is not exactly new. But we might still want to ask, why does the thought crop up so often and in such diverse quarters in the century in which Descartes writes? Is it mere chance? or perhaps intellectual vogue? I believe the answer is "no." The linkage of God with deceit – or non-deceit – corresponds (I shall argue) to an important shift in outlook on human beings that took place in Europe in the seventeenth century; a shift mirrored in the Grotean remark that we have just met; and mirrored, too, in a question that will preoccupy Descartes for an entire *Meditation*: has he a right to complain that God has not made him better than he is? But this is up the path; for the moment, let us stay with *Meditation One*, and continue to focus our sights on doubt and doubting.

There is, after all, one major difference between Descartes and his contemporaries. When Suárez or Grotius discuss God and deceit, they treat the subject largely as an intellectual matter: they consider arguments for and against, and come to the reasoned conclusion that God does not deceive, ever. Descartes, on the other hand, is not debating an abstract issue. The question is not whether God misleads human beings sometimes or never; but rather, whether God is deceiving him, Descartes, now and always ("*semper*," says our text above (p. 19)). Might he, Descartes, not be like the village clock ringing the wrong hour now, because he has been so rigged as to ring the wrong hour all the time? What is more, Descartes will not attempt to remove the worry at once through some argument showing its emptiness: on the contrary, he will bask in it for more than two *Meditations* and stop only when, were he to continue, he could advance no further in his quest. He does at some point (AT 7, 36; CSM 2, 25) call the deceiving God a "very tenuous and so to speak metaphysical" reason for doubting; but most of the time there is a much more personal and dramatic tone to the thought of that deceit.

In fact, the drama will get Descartes into trouble – with Dutch religious authorities. At both Utrecht and Leiden he will be accused of blasphemy for having so seriously supposed that God was a deceiver. Descartes has a standard reply to the charge.[10] There is a world of difference, he argues, between *supposing* something and *believing* it: unlike belief, supposition is a mere stance of the intellect, and involves no commitment of any kind on the part of the supposer. As we shall see up the road, commitment (or "assent," to use his word) is for Descartes a crucial element in the life of the mind; so it is perhaps not surprising that he should appeal to the fact of its absence when answering the charge of blasphemy. Whether the answer is sufficient is, of course, another matter. Think of Othello, the jealous husband who distrusts his wife even though she has never given him any ground for suspicion. Isn't that Descartes' situation *vis-à-vis* God? Unlike his own sense-perceptions or dreams, he has never caught God deceiving him; so suspicion of God is no more justified by the adage of distrust than is suspicion of Desdemona. Are we not inclined to pass judgment on Othello? "We have contempt for a man who is jealous of his wife, because this indicates that he does not love her in the right way and that he has a bad opinion of himself or of her. I say that he does not love her in the right way, for if he truly loved her he would not have any inclination to distrust her." Who writes this? – Descartes, talking about "blamable" (*blâmable*) jealousy in article 169 of the *Passions of the Soul* (AT 11, 458; CSM 1, 390). In 1676, Leiden forbade discussion of the deceiving God hypothesis.[11]

In thinking about the deceitful God it may be useful to begin with the verdict passed by David Hume, one hundred years after the *Meditations*: "Cartesian doubt, were it ever possible to be attained by any human creature (as it plainly is not) would be entirely incurable."[12] Let's leave the matter of incurability for later, and focus on the other charge – that the doubt "plainly" cannot "be attained by any human creature."

Concentrate on the first word, the adverb. A seemingly plain way to voice the deceiving God hypothesis is the formula I used for couching his earlier doubts about the shape of towers or the posture of his body. Let it now be about the sum of two plus three – an example that Descartes himself gives when he introduces the new doubt (see the text I quoted two pages ago). The words will go like this, then: "I am sure that two plus three equals five; but perhaps God is deceiving me; so perhaps two plus three does not equal five." No problem with the first clause: what could be more clear and distinct (to use Descartes' favorite adjectives) than my grasp of that simple sum? But questions arise at once when we go beyond it, especially with the last clause, the "perhaps-not" sentence. Uncategorical though it sounds, am I able to assert it at all – able *psychologically*? Am I able to say that perhaps two plus three does not equal five – not just speak or write the words, but genuinely mean them? We have once again stumbled onto the clash between "of course yes" and "perhaps no", but this time in a situation where the "of course" feels enormously strong: can we still, in *that* situation, entertain the thought that "perhaps no"?

In one important text, Descartes denies that we can:

> Some perceptions are so transparently clear and at the same time so simple that we can never think of them without believing them to be true. . . . We cannot doubt them unless we think of them; but we cannot think of them

without at the same time believing they are true. Hence we cannot doubt them without at the same time believing them to be true; that is, we can never doubt them.

. . . Nor is it an objection that such truths might appear false to God or to an angel; for the evidence of our perception will not allow us to hear anyone who makes up this kind of story.[13]

Assume that "two plus three equals five" fits the bill of being a transparently clear (*perspicua*) perception; then – says our text – we can never doubt it, or even hear (*audire*) the suggestion that we might be tricked about it by a deceiving God. For doubting one's perception involves thinking of it; and when the perception is transparently clear, mere thought entails belief.

Still, the moral to be drawn needn't be Hume's – that the deceiving-God hypothesis plainly cannot be entertained; but rather, that it cannot be entertained plainly. We need more complex strategies of distrust; and in fact, in the *Meditations* Descartes offers two, though one of them only fleetingly. "It will be a good plan to turn my will squarely in the opposite direction and deceive myself (*me ipsum fallere*) by pretending for a time that these former opinions are utterly false and imaginary," says *Meditation One* soon after the deceiving God comes onto the scene (AT 7, 22; CSM 2, 15). Here is the first scenario, then: deceive ourselves.

Even though it is a familiar feature of our lives, self-deception is not easy to conceptualize. Think of the jealous husband (Othello?) who brings himself to distrust his wife, while at bottom he knows full well that she is in love with him. We seem to have a partition of the ego here – into, on the one hand, a self that knows the truth; and, on the other, a self that represses this knowledge and wallows in suspicion. A similar partition, then, would occur when we brood about the deceiving God – between an ego aware of two plus three, and an ego that represses this awareness and thinks that perhaps God has so made him – etc., etc. Of course, "repression", in this modern sense, is not a seventeenth-century term; but Descartes seems pretty close to voicing the idea when he speaks of "turning [his] will squarely in the opposite direction." Granted, the mental dynamics are different – turning away rather than pushing down; but the upshot seems the same.

As far as I know, the appeal to self-deception as a model for entertaining the thought of God's deceit occurs only in the few lines that I have quoted, so we should perhaps not make too much of it. There is, however, another scenario of mental partition that Descartes describes at greater length in the *Meditations*, near the start of *Meditation Three* (AT 7, 36; CSM 2, 25):

Whenever the preconceived thought of God's supreme power comes to me, I cannot but admit that it would be easy for him, if he so wished, to bring it about that I go wrong even in what I think I see most clearly with my mind's eye. Yet when I turn to the things themselves which I think I perceive very clearly, I am so convinced by them that I burst out: "let whoever can deceive me, he will never bring it about that . . . two and three added together make more or less than five, or any such thing in which I see a manifest contradiction."

Descartes is reporting in himself incompatible beliefs. When he entertains the thought of God's power, he believes that this God could deceive him about any proposition, however evident; but when he contemplates one such proposition (for example "two plus three equals five"), he feels sure that he could not be deceived about it by any God, however powerful. What we have here is one type of inner conflict – not someone at the same time divided between two opposite views, but someone at different and specifiable-by-himself times fully committed to each of two opposite views.

Such a predicament is not extraordinary. In Strindberg's play *The Father*, Adolf, the hero, believes that women – all women – are infinitely deceitful, and can feign love for a man when in fact they feel none. Given this and (end-of-nineteenth-century) facts of human physiology, no man can ever know for certain that the child whom he takes to be his natural daughter really is his daughter. Now, true enough, Adolf acknowledges that at various moments of his conjugal life he has been unable to resist the conviction that his wife loved him – and for all he knows, he may again in the future be unable to resist – but he reflects that his inability to doubt his wife on such occasions can only be taken as yet another proof of women's immense ability to deceive. Eventually, Adolf commits suicide, and here of course the parallel with *Meditation One* comes to an end – as we know, Descartes' quandary had a happier outcome.

What the Strindbergian analogue does bring out, though, is that in conflicts of this kind a person's thoughts must be individuated according to the time of their occurrence. The conflict features two episodes or series of episodes: the time or times of passion, when Adolf is unable to distrust his wife; and the time or times of doubt, when he has the conviction of infinite feminine guile. But now, turning back to Descartes, there arises a question. It is unnatural to suppose that people have no memory of their past thoughts and convictions even as they are in the grip of a contrary conviction; so at the very moment when Adolf believes that no man can ever be certain of his wife, he is likely to remember moments when he nonetheless did feel certain of her. And here, Descartes' fate may seem perforce different. The memory of a moment of passion need not be at all like feeling that passion again: to remember love is only very rarely to relive it. But is there a similar distance between remembering a Cartesian certainty and feeling it? Don't forget, according to Descartes there are those "utterly clear" perceptions, whose mere thought is sufficient to generate belief. Well, what happens with remembrance in their case? Does the memory of having been certain that two plus three equaled five involve the thought that two plus three equals five, and therefore the certainty that two plus three equals five? If yes, Cartesian doubt requires some sort of amnesia.

Of course, Descartes need not say "yes." And anyhow, he has another method of distancing yesterday's acquiescences from today's distrust. Return to the quote from *Meditation Three*, cited above: "it would be easy for him . . . to bring it about that I go wrong even in what I think I see most clearly with my mind's eye." Note the distant manner in which Descartes states what a deceiving God could deceive him about – no instance is offered, only a general description. And while instances are mentioned in the *Meditation One* text that ushers in the deceiving God (look back again at p. 19 above), they are mentioned only indirectly: "May I not similarly be mistaken every time I add two and three or count the sides of a square" – the doubt is made to bear on the mental acts of adding and counting, and Descartes never actually articulates the propositions, connected with these acts, that God might make him mistaken about.

So the thought of the deceiving God can be entertained in a roundabout way: I can tell myself that perhaps God has so made me that I am mistaken even in those matters where I feel the most sure, and go into no further detail. It is also worth pointing out that only *some* of my certainties are such that they can be questioned only in this indirect manner: simple arithmetic, and general truisms like "what is done cannot be undone" or "I am not nothing, when I think that I am something" – these are Descartes' own examples. Other basic convictions, I can doubt quite straightforwardly. I can say for example "I am sure I have a body; but perhaps God is deceiving me; so perhaps I have no body"; or "I am sure there are other people in the world; but perhaps . . . etc., etc." In these (as we shall see) crucially important cases, I can in the same breath confess my certainty and declare my suspicions. Let me call those: *directly doubtable* certainties.

Adolf commits suicide, Descartes does not. This doesn't mean, however, that for Descartes the thought of the deceiving God is not a searing experience: "It feels as though I have fallen unexpectedly into a deep whirlpool which tumbles me around so that I can neither stand on the bottom nor swim up to the top" – that is how *Meditation Two* begins. *Meditation One* had ended on a similar note, conveyed by a different image. Descartes compared himself to a prisoner who enjoys an imaginary freedom while asleep, and so induces himself to go on dreaming: the oneiric freedom in this instance is of course freedom from doubt. Notice, incidentally, that in this image of the prisoner, self-deception appears once again: self-deception exercised in making oneself not wake up to a painful reality. Amusingly, the deceit now works in the opposite direction – as a means *not* to entertain the thought of the deceitful God.

Be that as it may, one must wonder why Descartes chooses to remain in that obsessive mood for so long, till *Meditation Four* in fact.[14] The main reason is simple. Remember, the supposition that God has so made him as to be always mistaken enables Descartes to separate two kinds of certainties – those where, thanks to the supposition, he can say "perhaps no" even as he articulates one of them; and those where, despite the supposition, he cannot. He can say "perhaps I have no body"; but he cannot *really* say "perhaps two plus three does not equal five." In my words, this is the distinction between certainties that are directly doubtable and certainties that are not. Well, Descartes will devote an entire *Meditation*, the *Second*, to exploring this divide insofar as it applies to certaintics that we have about *ourselves* – about the kind of creatures we are. And from the divide between certainties, he will draw far-reaching conclusions about what these certainties are about – about the kind of creatures we are. But this is for later.

Unreliable senses, dreams, deceiving God: these are the grounds for doubt that have been presented so far. Before leaving *Meditation One*, however, I want to cast a quick glance at three other grounds that Descartes offers there. They appear only fleetingly; but each will, in its own way, have an interesting fate.

Here is the first:

> What reason could I have for denying that these hands, this body, are mine unless I should compare myself to those insane men whose brains are so damaged by destructive vapours arising from the black bile that they keep asserting that they are kings (when they are destitute), that they are wearing purple (when they are naked), that they have heads of clay, or are pumpkins, or are blown out of glass? But they are madmen, and I should appear no less mad if I took their case to apply to me.

This occurs early on, soon after the doubt about the shapes of distant towers. Descartes has just acknowledged that distrust of the reliability of his eyesight will not justify him in doubting very much: after all, his eyes have deceived him only about matters small or distant. What about his certainty that he is now sitting by the fire, wearing a gown, holding a sheet of paper? Well – and here comes our text (AT 7, 19; CSM 2, 13) – could he not be like those *insani* who take themselves to be . . . etc., etc?

Two facts are striking about this supposition. One is that it is entertained ultra-briefly – exactly the one sentence we have here; and dismissed even more briefly – the sybilline second sentence of our text. We never hear of madness again in the *Meditations*. The second, and perhaps related, fact is that these two sentences attracted no attention among academic readers of Descartes – until a few decades ago. In 1961, in his *Histoire de la folie à l'âge classique*, Michel Foucault adduced the curt dismissal by Descartes of the madness-hypothesis as further of evidence of a phenomenon which he argued was one of the striking events of the early seventeenth century – "*le Grand Renfermement*," "the Great Confinement": throughout Western Europe, people deemed insane were shut into institutions of detainment, and silenced.

Though only a passing remark,[15] this assessment elicited a lengthy reply from Jacques Derrida, who offered a much more minimalist reading of the passage.[16] According to Derrida, Descartes' abandonment of the hypothesis that he might be insane is a move of no philosophic significance: the hypothesis is given up simply because the supposition that he might be dreaming is a more convenient substitute; more convenient, in that dreams, unlike madness, are a condition with which everyone is familiar; and also, perhaps, because the imputation of dreaming will be less offensive to the ordinary reader. In fact, that is the reason for the switch given in Descartes' unpublished dialogue that parallels the *Meditations*, the *Search for Truth* (AT 10, 511; CSM 2, 407).

As one might expect, Foucault replied to the rejoinder,[17] arguing again for the non-deflationary view: to even suppose that he might be mad would, in the eyes of a seventeenth-century reader, disqualify Descartes altogether from pursuing his philosophic enterprise, since it would, so to speak, brand him with endemic irrationality. Both Derrida and Foucault have had followers. Given the sparse and sybilline text, there is faint hope for resolution, and ample room for speculation. This has indeed occurred – one more symptom, perhaps, of the remarkable ability of Descartes' prose to generate wonder and discussion.

The doubt that I am now about to mention has had almost the opposite fate: undeserved notoriety. It occurs a bit later, toward the end of *Meditation One* (AT 7, 22; CSM 2, 15); and is offered as a substitute for the deceiving God hypothesis. Perhaps mindful of possible charges of blasphemy, Descartes writes:

> I will suppose therefore that not God, who is supremely good and the source of truth, but some evil genius of the utmost power and cunning has employed all his energies in order to deceive me. I shall think that the sky, the air, the earth, colours, shapes, sounds and all external things are merely the delusions of dreams which he has devised to ensnare my judgement.

In Latin, the words are "*malignus genius*"; in French, "*malin génie*"; and in standard English translation, "evil genius."[18] The malignant, or cunning (*callidus*), deceiver will be mentioned three more times in the next few pages – the middle mention occurring at an admittedly important moment, the so-called *cogito* argument near the beginning of *Meditation Two* (AT 7, 25; CSM 2, 17). After that, silence: we never meet the demon again. We are not told how he disappears, and are left to presume (as does Bourdin,[19] the only objector to have noticed his coming onto the stage at all) that a benevolent God would "curb" (*coercere*) his activities. So he is not an enduring presence in the *Meditations*.

Yet astonishingly, it is to him – not God – that posterity has given pride of place in Descartes' pantheon of deceit. One might almost say that the demon's greatest achievement has been to usurp God's position – to have posterity transfer to *him* all the powers of deception that Descartes attributed, albeit briefly and hypothetically, to God. Like "Plato's Forms," "Descartes' Evil Genius" is now philosophic lore; and one might wonder why. After all, unlike Descartes, we today have no worries about blasphemy.

Perhaps it's simply glamour. I take it that the most obvious difference between the deceiving God and the cunning demon is that one is well-intentioned while the other is not: God would make us see roses and blue skies where there are only colorless atoms; the demon would do the opposite. Now, sadly perhaps, it is a fact of human nature that malevolent deceivers are more interesting to spectators than benevolent ones. The Evil Genius has distinguished company in the seventeenth century – think only of Iago or Don Juan[20] – while one is hard put to find *any* well-meaning liar to match their renown, then or at some other time. And of course, in a sense it matters very little whom posterity remembers in connection with Descartes and deceit – Genius or deceiving God. Both are but passing specters; neither, it will turn out, can exist.

Yet in another sense, some important things are lost in the shuffle. When the demon is taken as the chief perpetrator of deceit, concerns that are very relevant to the subsequent course of the *Meditations* disappear. One is the problem of benevolent deception. Though perhaps less glamorous than its wicked counterpart, that brand is well worth thinking about – especially in connection with Descartes' doubt. Why shouldn't God, out of sheer kindness, have so made us that we see roses where there are only atoms? Descartes will be repeatedly quizzed on that point, and, as we shall see, his answers leave something to be desired. Also lost in the switch is the issue of fabrication. Exactly how would the cunning demon ensnare us? It would be by casting a spell, or hypnotizing us, putting as it were *dreams* into our heads (this is Descartes' word: see text on p. 26). That is of course an intelligible technique, but more complicated than God's way would be were *he* to deceive us. God, who is our maker, would simply have made us in the first place like clocks that always ring the wrong time – rigged pieces of machinery. Nor is it just a matter of simplicity. The theme of making, crafting, fabricating, looms very large in the *Meditations* – it will turn out to be at the center of God's relation with human beings. We should not miss the opening bars through being fixated on the Evil Genius.

As it happens, that same theme resonates loudly in the one further ground for massive doubt that appears in the *First Meditation*. It comes after the deceiving God, and like the Evil Genius, is offered as a sort of variant (AT 7, 21; CSM 2, 14):

> Perhaps there will be some who would rather deny the existence of so pow-erful a God than believe that everything else is uncertain. Let us not argue with them, but grant that everything said about God is a fiction. According to their supposition, then, I have arrived at my present state by fate or chance or a continuous chain of events, or by some other means. Since mistakes and errors seem to be some sort of imperfection, the less powerful they make my original cause, the more likely it is that I am so imperfect as to be mistaken all the time.

The supposition voiced here has no set name in Cartesian literature: let me call it the "blind-force" hypothesis. Suppose I have been put together not by God but by some blind force, as a mound of pebbles might be assembled by the tide on a beach; then there is all the more rea-son to believe that I am a greatly imperfect creature – so imperfect, in fact, as never to be right about anything.

Of course we, post-Darwinians, have more complex views than Descartes about the interplay of chance and perfection – we are less ready to regard chance as leading necessarily to maladaptation.[21] But we would still agree, I think, with the adage that subtends his argument, namely:

> the less accomplished the maker, the less accomplished the product.

(Where Descartes writes "powerful" and "perfect," I have for the sake of simplicity put the same adjective on both sides of the equation.) Let me call what has just been enunciated, an "axiom of fabrication." It's commonsense enough: we do not expect an apprentice to make as good a watch as will a master craftsman. However, as we shall see, the seven-teenth century and Descartes (and perhaps we, too) apply the axiom not just to the making of mechanical contraptions such as watches; no, that century (and perhaps we, too) extend it to what may seem at first to be a very different sort of product – the ideas that human beings have. And in that special context, the axiom will play a pivotal role in the *Meditations*. But again, that is for later; we are, for the moment, just hearing the opening bars.

One final question: exactly who are the "some" that Descartes is addressing when he offers the blind-force argument? (look back to the first line: "there will be some (*nonnulli*) who . . ."). In the *Meditation* he affixes no label; but he will do so when he restates that doubt in the *Sixth Replies* (AT 7, 428; CSM 2, 289):

> the less power the atheist assigns to the author of his being, the more he will have occasion to worry (*occasionem dubitandi*) that his nature may be so imperfect that he is mistaken even in what seems most evident to him.

Atheists, whether real or imaginary, are of course the routine whipping boys of the seventeenth century – everyone seeks to distance him- or herself from them. In Descartes, though, the whipping has motives deeper than routine: it stems from a desire to defend the integrity of the doubt. He has to parry attacks on two fronts. On one side are what we might call the doubt-dramatizers – the (proto-Humean) critics who say that the doubt, if held seriously, is so damaging as to be incurable. But there is also the opposite side – call them the doubt-skeptics – opponents who say that, so far from being devastating and incurable, the doubt of the deceiving God is a pseudo-worry, no real ailment at all. These skeptics come in various guises, the most straightforward being the one addressed here – someone who claims immunity from the doubt on the ground that he doesn't believe in any God, let alone one who deceives. As we see, Descartes has a ready reply, based on the axiom of fabrication: the unbeliever, he answers, exposes himself to an even more virulent form of self-distrust – doubt of all his faculties.

We shall hear a good deal more about trust and distrust as we pursue the *Meditations*.

me and others

The *Second Meditation* will teach two lessons: one, that I know my mind better than I know my body; and two, that I know my mind better than I know yours. The first is announced in the title, *Of the nature of the human mind; that it is better known than the body*. And the second is the corollary of a disturbing thought that strikes Descartes near the end of the *Meditation* (AT 7, 32; CSM 2, 21): "I happened to look through the window . . . and say that I see men: yet what do I see, except hats and coats that may conceal automata?" This naturally prompts the question: how do I know what goes on in your mind, when I am not even certain that you have one?

Faced with this Cartesian program, a reader may be inclined to say "so what?" After all, the lessons that Descartes wishes to impart look like truisms. All sorts of things are happening inside my skin right now of which I know nothing; but if I am bored by your conversation, I can hardly escape noting. On the other hand, if I bore you, I may very well never find out – you may be a master of disguise. So yes, my mind is more present to me than my body, and more present to me than your mind. But as we might guess, Descartes' program goes beyond these simple facts; it aims at something grander, a description of the *nature* of the human mind – that's what the title says too. Nor should we take this word "nature" for granted: exactly what is being sought by Descartes under that label? We should also observe that there are plenty of truisms going the other way. Think not of simple feelings like boredom, but more complicated ones like, say, having low self-esteem. Suppose that that is my mental state right now: am I bound to know? Could you not, in fact, be more aware of my being in that state than I am? So it looks as though, in at least some instances, my mind is better known to you than to me. These are tricky matters; so we should not only plan to have a clearer vision of Descartes' general aim – discovering the nature of the human mind; but also examine how the doctrine copes with apparent counter-examples.

The first step of his progress is known well enough: it is the *cogito*, the Mona Lisa of philosophy. Remember, Descartes has fallen into a deep

whirlpool, where he can neither stand on the bottom nor swim to the top
– that is his own image of the state of mind that the hypothesis of the
deceiving God has induced. Does this mean that he must whirl forever?
No:

[A]
There is a deceiver of supreme power and supreme cunning who is deliberately and constantly deceiving me. In that case I, too, undoubtedly exist – if
he is deceiving me. And let him deceive me as much as he can, he will
never bring it about that I am nothing as long as I think that I am something. So after considering everything very thoroughly I must finally conclude that this proposition, *I am, I exist*, is necessarily true whenever I
state it or conceive it in my mind.
   But I do not yet understand well enough what this "I" is . . .

For the sake of future reference, I call this text "[A]." This is AT 7, 25;
CSM 2, 17 – you will look in vain for the canonical formula; it is
nowhere in the *Meditations*.

I shall assume that this absence has no philosophic significance. "*Je
pense donc je suis*" occurred at a comparable moment in the *Discourse*
(AT 6, 32; CSM 1, 127); so will "*cogito ergo sum*" in the *Principles* (Part
1, art. 7: AT 8a, 7; CSM 1, 195); and in all discussions Descartes seems to
regard the formula, whether Latin or French, as an apt expression of his
thought.[1] So let me put the reasoning in a simpler form than the complex *Meditation* passage that I have just quoted, and more in line with
the universally received dictum. It will go like this: to be deceived, one
must have thoughts; and to have thoughts, one must exist. Assume that
God or an evil genius is deceiving me; then I have thoughts; then I exist.
I think therefore I am.

But is that gloss really fair? or does it encumber the *cogito* with an extra
premise that in fact damages its soundness? The problem lies with the
general first proposition – about one's needing to exist in order to think,
and needing to think in order to be deceived. It looks obvious enough;
but if we suppose, as we are meant to, that God deceives even about
what is most obvious, could he not be deceiving precisely about *that*?
We now appear to be faced with a dilemma: either maintain that the *cogito* is indubitable because it does not require that general premise; or say
that it requires it, but this takes nothing away from its indubitability. As
you can imagine, Descartes was quizzed on this point;[2] he replied; comments ensued; comments upon the comments; etc., etc. Rather than add
to the corpus, I shall take a different tack.

Ask yourself, why is Descartes challenged in this way? The answer is
plain: if we are to accept that he has attained a first truth that escapes the

tentacles of the deceiving God, a truth furthermore that is, as he proclaims, the most certain of all truths,[3] then we must make sure that it really does escape the doubt – sure that he, Descartes, has not been taken in by the deceiver. In a famous image (*Seventh Replies*: AT 7, 481; CSM 2, 324), he compares himself to the owner of a basket of apples, of which he knows some to be rotten: to prevent the rot from spreading, the safest course is to empty the whole basket and then put the apples back one by one, examining each to make sure that it is unspoiled and healthy. Well, here he is at the beginning of *Meditation Two*, about to put the first apple back: the more we probe for blemishes, the more certain we shall be of the apple's wholesomeness and integrity. From that perspective, Descartes fully deserves a guarded and critical attitude on the part of his readers – one that leads them to raise questions such as the one I mentioned in the previous paragraph. Here is another, in the same vein: is Descartes really entitled to use the first person – to utter "*I* think"? After all, what he has experienced is a sequence of thoughts: for him now to say "I think," does he not need the further clause that thoughts require a thinker? And could not a deceiving God deceive him about *that*?

Given that the *Second Meditation* comes after the *First*, questions of this kind are perfectly in order. But might it not be useful to ask an altogether different sort of question, namely: what if *Meditation One* had *not* occurred? What if we did *not* have to regard the *cogito* as the first apple placed back into the basket, as the first proposition to stand up to the doubt? How would we feel about it then? This is not wild hypothetical pondering; the question is prompted by one simple thought. Remember, the dictum has universal fame; it has for centuries conveyed a message to people who in no way placed its significance in the fact that it stemmed the tide of the doubt – this for the simple reason that, almost certainly, they had never heard of the Cartesian doubt. Nor are they alone: odds are that we, readers of Descartes – perhaps even Descartes himself – hear that message too in some subliminal form. So why not don blinkers and try to look at the dictum through the eyes of the untutored viewer? We might gain valuable insight in the process.

For the sake of brevity, let me call the *cogito* as I presume it to be understood by philosophically innocent mortals, the "mundane" or "lay" *cogito*; and call the one that involves taking the *First Meditation* into account, the "cleric's" or "strict" *cogito*. About the mundane *cogito*, a few facts deserve notice.

The first bears on the central word *ergo* (or *donc*, or *therefore*). Suppose you are asked for a paraphrase of "I think therefore I am," you might well offer this one: "if I didn't think, I wouldn't (really) be."[4] If that gloss is accurate, it points to a curious fact, namely: the *therefore* of the mundane *cogito* is not the logician's *therefore* – it works, so to speak, in the opposite direction. Take the hallowed "Socrates is a man, so Socrates is mortal." This says that if Socrates were not mortal, he would not be a man; it does *not* say that if he were not a man, he would not be mortal – he might be a cat or a centaur. In standard logic, then, "*P* therefore *Q*" conveys the thought that if *Q* were not the case, then *P* would not be; and it does not convey the reverse. Yet that is precisely what the "*P* therefore *Q*" of the mundane *cogito* does convey – its proper paraphrase being (as we have just seen) "if *P* were not the case, then *Q* wouldn't be." So this must be a different *therefore*.

What is more, if you look around, that kind is not uncommon in ordinary speech. I am at a party, where a fellow guest behaves in an annoying fashion: he interrupts, monopolizes the conversation, is disagreeable and sarcastic. Afterwards, someone explains: "he has low self-esteem, so he is aggressive." The force of this remark can again be conveyed by an "if . . . then" statement, like "if he hadn't low self-esteem, he wouldn't be aggressive (in that way)." Again and for similar reasons, this is not the logicians' *so* or *therefore*; and, we might wonder, does it share a characteristic with the *therefore* of the lay person's *cogito*?

The answer is "yes." In both cases, the connecting adverb is used to tell one about the make-up of whoever is being talked about: we can paraphrase by saying something of the form "*x* is what really makes [me/him] *y*." The mundane *cogito* declares that thinking is what really makes me exist; and the diagnosis of the disagreeable guest says that low self-esteem is what really makes him so aggressive. If we want a label, let's say that we have here not the *logicians'*, but the *diagnosticians'*, "therefore."

This trait is closely linked with a second matter that deserves attention and is perhaps best approached by reflecting on the *cogito*'s magnetism, or inspirational power. A striking fact about the five words "I think therefore I am" (and their equivalents in the main European languages – I can't speak of others) is that they are so famous because, somehow, they invite *spoofing*. "I run therefore I am," "I shop therefore I am," "I am read therefore I am" – not a month passes without one's meeting a new specimen. The spoofs generally have a jocular tinge but, as we know, jokes don't just aim at amusement. So, we might ask, what is it about Descartes' sentence that provokes so many people into uttering it with a different first verb?[5] and what makes utterances of the form "I . . . therefore I am" natural vehicles for seemingly significant declarations?

Consider an example. Coming back from her daily exercise, a colleague exclaims: "I run therefore I am!" I know at once what to make of the remark. It says that running is not an activity in which she just happens to engage, or that is on a par with other occupations of hers. No, running is more important: if she did not run she wouldn't be the kind of person she is. In other words – and these are not innocent words – running is somehow *essential* to her being. Something else is true of my colleague's exclamation. Its words carry some sort of shock-value: what they declare essential looks outlandish at first, yet becomes understandable as one reflects. "What, *running*? – Sure, why not?" Also present, probably, is a chime of protest – protest against stereotyping: she – people – are more complex than the Cartesian adage makes them out to be.

What about the adage itself, then, the *cogito*: where lies *its* ring of provocation? Almost certainly it is in the exclusionary outlook, in the disdain of the life of the heart, that its words seem to express. "Intellect [the utterer is heard as saying] is what makes me properly human – not feelings, emotions or desires." We shall have to return to that contrast; but using a crude label, let me say that *intellectualism* is what the lay person hears as the main note of "I think therefore I am." We should remember this, as we turn to the cleric's version.

Back to *Meditation Two*, then, and its *cogito* uttered against the backdrop of the doubt. Here the speaker's immediate intent is less complex: he wishes to state a proposition that is undoubtedly true – to place that first apple back into the basket. Exactly what the apple is, is up to a point a matter of choice for the reader: we might take it to be "I think," or "I think therefore I am," or even (as Descartes seems to indicate in the *Meditation Two* version that I quoted above – my text [A]) "I am." It does not greatly matter. One fact to observe, though, is that for "I am" to appear on this list, we must take the connecting adverb in the *cogito*-formula to be the logician's *therefore* – and not, as before, the "diagnostic" one. What "*P* therefore *Q*" now conveys is that if *Q* were not the case, then *P* would not be: if Descartes did not exist, he would not be thinking at all.

Such is the *cogito* in its strict version. Yet as the *Meditation* unfolds, we are due for a surprise. We soon read (call it "text [B]"):

> Thought – this alone is inseparable from me. *I am, I exist*, that is certain. But for how long? For as long as I think. It might perhaps even happen that if I entirely stopped thinking, I should at once altogether stop being. I admit here nothing but what is necessarily true. Strictly, then, I am only a thing that thinks, i.e. a mind, or intelligence, or intellect, or reason.

This is AT 7, 27; CSM 2, 18 – less than two pages after our text [A], the original *cogito* passage. Given the deliberate echo "I am, I exist," plus the claim that Descartes is admitting only what is "necessarily true," it seems reasonable to regard this text as a follow-up of the earlier one.

However, if it *is* a follow-up it is certainly not an obvious one – especially when you take in the sentence about what "might perhaps happen." Omit the perhaps-words for the moment: how is it that Descartes, having started from the fact that he would stop thinking if he stopped being (remember, that is what the cleric's *cogito* says) has now come to the view that he would stop being if he stopped thinking? Could it be that he, too, is hearing the siren song of the other *cogito*, the mundane one? That suspicion is only made stronger when we look at the final sentence of our text – the one about what he, Descartes, "strictly speaking" *is*: "I am only a thing that thinks [*res cogitans*] i.e. a mind [*mens*], or intelligence [*animus*], or intellect [*intellectus*], or reason [*ratio*]." It would be hard to find a more emphatic statement of the intellectualist manifesto that the lay person hears in the *cogito*. So we should ask ourselves: how is it that Descartes' path and the lay person's – which seemed so divergent at first – have come to coincide?

Up to a point the answer is simple: the convergence is an outcome of the doubt.[6] Having discovered one proposition that stemmed the tide, Descartes now wants to extend the dyke, or (to change the image) put more apples back into the basket. But of course each apple must be healthy and known to be such – the test of knowledge, here, being one's *in*ability to add "perhaps not." If I can say "I am certain that . . . ; but God may be deceiving me; so perhaps not . . . ," then I cannot truly be said to know. We are back to our distinction between two kinds of certainties – those that are directly doubtable, and those that are not. It will now turn out that one crucial item belongs to the directly doubtable kind.

Return once more to the *cogito*. Having discovered *that* he is, Descartes asks himself *what* he is (this passage comes between [A] and [B]):

[C]
What shall I then say that I am, when I am supposing that there is some supremely powerful and, if I may say so, malignant deceiver, who is deliberately trying to trick me in every way he can? Can I assert that I possess even the most insignificant of all the attributes I have just said belong to the nature of the body? I scrutinize, think, go over them again, but find none that I can say is mine.[7]

Why does Descartes find no bodily attribute he can call his own? Answer: because he is able to suppose that he has no body at all. We have here one of the key tenets of the system – that we can directly doubt the existence of our body. Each of us is able to say, meaning it: "I think I have a body; but perhaps God is deceiving me; so perhaps I have none." No argument is ever given for our ability to say this; it is simply one of the chief axioms of the *Meditations*.

Given that axiom and the consequence Descartes draws from it – that he is not entitled, at this point, to ascribe any bodily feature to himself

– his self-description in text [B] takes on a different hue. When he writes that "strictly, I am only a thing that thinks," the word "strictly" (*præcise*) means: "so far as I am entitled to say at this moment"; perhaps later, he will be entitled to say more. Descartes makes it quite clear that he is offering only an interim description of himself (AT 7, 27; CSM 2, 18):

[D]
May it not be that these very things which I am supposing to be nothing because they are unknown to me, are in fact no different from this "I" that I know? I cannot tell, and shall not argue the point for the moment, since I can make judgments only about the things that are known to me.

What Descartes is now supposing to be nothing – his body – may in fact be no different from what he now knows to be something – his mind. And he will stress the possible linkage between body and mind even more strongly on the next page (AT 7, 28; CSM 2, 19), when he asks again what being a thing-that-thinks amounts to: it involves *inter alia*, he replies, being a thing-that-feels (*res sentiens*).[8] So the narrow intellectualism displayed in the remark that he is just "a mind, an intellect, a reason" is no more than a provisional stance forced on Descartes by the doubt of the deceiving God. It may not outlive that doubt – so much is made emphatically clear to the reader. But of course, it may outlive the doubt too.

There still remains the espousal of the mundane *cogito*, inherent in the remark that if he stopped thinking he might stop being: how did *that* come about? Perhaps the best way to trace the steps is to look again at the title of our *Meditation*, and ask what we have learnt so far about the topics announced in it. What have we learnt about the nature of the human mind? And what, about its being better known than the body?

Well, we have found *one* respect in which we are better acquainted with our mind than we are with our body: we can doubt that we have the one, while we cannot doubt that we have the other. A more dramatic (and first-person singular) way of expressing this asymmetry would be to say that "thought alone is inseparable from me": this is our text [B]. We should take good notice of the adjective – "inseparable." On the one hand, inseparability is connected with the doubt. Suppose I now think that I am walking: the *thinking* that I walk is inseparable from me – I cannot doubt that I think as I do. By contrast, I can doubt that I do as I think – I might be dreaming, or even not have a body at all; so, walking *is* separable from me. In the *Fifth Replies* Descartes will wonder whether he might have said, instead of *cogito*, "*ambulo ergo sum*", "I walk therefore I am" – an early spoof, obviously. No, he answers, he could not, because he could not "infer the existence of a body that walks" (AT 7, 352; CSM 2, 244).

But inseparability is also a bridge to Descartes' other topic announced in the title – the account of his mind's nature. Go back once more to our text [B.] Soon after the sentence about what is inseparable, we read the words: "if I entirely stopped thinking, I should at once altogether stop being." Fair enough: if high wind is inseparable from rainstorms, then if the wind has gone, so has the storm. Another way of expressing this tie would be to say that it is in the nature of storms that they should have winds; likewise, it is in my nature that I should have thoughts. A thing's nature, in that sense, is a feature or set of features without which that thing would simply not exist.

So let us look back. How have the two *cogito*s – the cleric's and the mundane – come to meet? Answer: the cleric's version, conjoined with the dogma of the separability of the body, promptly yielded the conclusion that Descartes' nature was to think, which is what the lay person, too, takes the *cogito* to convey – though, granted, a little less strictly. When my colleague exclaims "I run, therefore I am", she doesn't mean that if she stopped running she would really stop living; but only, that if she stopped running she would stop *really* living – she would stop leading the kind of existence that brings out her full potential as a person. So there is a more complicated aura to her "I am"; more complicated, presumably, than to Descartes' – though who knows? Remember, in these post-*cogito* pages we've found that plethora of *perhaps*'s (our text [B]), plus the warning that things may look different from higher up the slope (text [D]). So this is not the last word.

But is it even the first? We have now been told about the nature of something, or someone – Descartes. He asked, "what am I?" and found that his nature was to think; he is a thinking thing. But what the title of our *Meditation* promised was an account of the nature not of an individual, but of the human mind. Nor is Descartes in any way confusing the two: his aim, he tells us in the middle of the *Meditation* (AT 7, 28; CSM 2, 19) is to make sure that his mind "perceives its own nature as distinctly as possible". Well, what perception has it achieved, or will it achieve?

It is not easy to say. For one thing, the second half of the *Meditation* has an odd impressionistic quality. Much of it is devoted to the discussion of an elusive example, the so-called piece of wax; and somehow there never comes a point where the reader can say with confidence: "Ah, here is Descartes' pronouncement of what the nature of the human mind is." So the temptation is great to import texts from elsewhere – and now of course, much is a matter of decision. Another problem is that Descartes, though again not saying so outright, might be using a more complex notion of "nature" than the one we have identified so far. Let me consider this last matter first; and I, too, shall be looking elsewhere for clues.

If you reflect, one word has been strangely absent from our *Meditation* – a certain synonym. When Descartes said (see text [B]) that if he did not think, he would not exist, he could have written – could he not? – that thinking was *essential* to his existing. We commonly use the word "essential" to designate a property without which the thing that owns it would not be; and perhaps less often, we use the corresponding noun, *essence*, in the same sense: we might say, for example, that it is in the essence of rainstorms that high winds blow during the course of them. So understood, *essence* is a close synonym of a word that occurs importantly in the title of our *Meditation*, namely *nature*. In fact, Descartes often conjoins the two and writes "nature or essence";[9] but not in *Meditation Two* – here, the synonym never appears. The omission is doubtless deliberate: perhaps it is simply to keep out words with a philosophical past, at this stage anyway.

Meditation Six, on the other hand, will involve much discussion of the "essence of the mind"; and the *Principles* – the tome intended for schools – in fact offer a definition of the word (Part 1, art. 53: AT 8a, 25; CSM 1, 210): "Each substance has one principal property which constitutes its nature and essence, and to which all its other properties are referred." This is a much more restrictive notion. As now understood, the essence or nature of a thing is not simply a feature without whose presence the thing would not exist; it is a feature that is "referred to" (today we might say "implied") by *every* inherent feature of that thing. Obviously in this sense, high wind is not essential to rain-storms: many commotions that happen in the course of them – thunder, lightning – do not seem to imply the presence of wind in any way.

Although it is nowhere explicitly stated, let us suppose that this stricter notion of *nature* is already at work in *Meditation Two* when Descartes seeks to make his mind "perceive its own nature as distinctly as possible." In that event, how should we expect him to proceed? The most likely route would be to list all sorts of mental activities or experiences, as disparate as possible, and then point to a feature, or features, that they all share. Let us look.

Here are the lines that immediately follow Descartes' announcement of the project to make his mind perceive its own nature as distinctly as possible:

[E]
What then am I? A thing that thinks. And what is that? A thing that doubts, understands, affirms, wants, doesn't want, and also imagines and feels. These are many things – if they all belong to me. But why wouldn't

they? Is it not I myself who now doubts everything, who nonetheless understands some things, who affirms that this one thing is true, denies everything else, desires to know more, doesn't want to be deceived, imagines many things even involuntarily, and feels many things as though they came through the senses?

This is AT 7, 28; CSM 2, 19. Descartes will continue in this vein a little longer, but surely the drift is clear. We are presented with a contrast between, on the one hand, a variety of mental activities or experiences – doubting, desiring, feeling, etc., and, on the other, a single feature they all share – that of being the activity of a certain *I*: "is it not I myself (*ego ipse*) who now . . . doubts . . . desires . . . feels . . . ?" So it does look as though Descartes takes the search for the nature of the mind to be the search for a feature that all mental activities have in common.

But what feature, exactly? Here again we might hesitate, because there are at least two ways to read the rhetorical question "is it not I myself who . . . ?" This might simply amount to the assertion that doubt, or feeling, or desire, do not occur without there being *someone* whose doubt or feeling or desire they are: in my case, it is me – *ego ipse*. Speaking more impersonally and calling (as Descartes does) all these mental activities "thoughts," one might sum up this view via the dictum:

There is no thought without a thinker.

On the other hand, Descartes might be putting forward a more exposed thesis. He might be saying that whenever he doubts anything or desires anything or feels anything, this involves his somehow having the idea of himself. Now, *that* is far from a truism. The claim is uncontroversial for wants or desires – how could we voice any without using a personal pronoun? For example: "I want to go running": how else to say it? It is another matter, though, for some of the other mental acts on Descartes' list: if I muse that perhaps the clock-tower isn't round, must I – deep down – be saying something like "I doubt that the clock-tower is round"? And if shiveringly I grunt "Brrr, it's cold!", does this perforce amount to "I feel cold"? Is there always a reference to myself, whether spoken or not? That view, too, can be summed up in a formula:

There is no thought without thought of oneself.

So the question is: does Descartes endorse just the first dictum, or also the second? The answer is almost certainly that he endorses both. For that is almost certainly the conclusion we are meant to draw from the case-study which follows our passage [E] and occupies the final third of the *Meditation*. I now turn to the "piece of wax."

It begins at AT 7, 30; CSM 2, 20.

> Let us take this wax. It has just been removed from the honeycomb; it has
> not yet lost the taste of its honey; it retains some of the scent of the flowers
> from which it was gathered . . .

The story will unfold over four pages, together with morals drawn from
it; it often has a fickle allusive quality, typically Cartesian – plain first
appearance, yet glimpses of a deeper hinterland; it has aroused much discussion, beginning with two of the *objectors*, Hobbes and Gassendi;[10]
I hope that my cursory account does no injustice to its intricacies.

Here is our wax, then, fresh from the honeycomb; but now we bring it
near a fire. Naturally, it turns liquid, loses its smell and color, and everything about it looks and feels different. Yet we still speak of *it*, the wax:
"The same wax remains; no one denies it; no one thinks otherwise."
What makes that thought possible? It cannot be information received
through the senses – nothing they tell us has remained constant. What is
it, then? Descartes canvasses a number of possibilities, and eventually
comes to the conclusion that what leads us to speak of *the* wax, to regard
it as still the same, is a "perception by the mind alone" (*sola mente
percip[itur]*) (AT 7, 31; CSM 2, 21). As it stands, that is of course just a
formula; we need to know what the key words mean. To explain,
Descartes will appeal to a contrast of which he is fond, and for which he
is notorious – the contrast between human beings and animals.

In the "piece of wax," that appeal is in fact ultra-brief, barely more
than a mention (AT 7, 32; CSM 2, 22); so in what follows, I shall at times
be elaborating on the actual text. One might put matters like this.
Confronted with our wax a dog may very well, like us, smell an odor or
see a color; but these are in its case *unattributed* perceptions: unlike us,
the dog does not experience what it sees or smells as qualities *of* something. It does not do so, because the very notion of a thing or object is
beyond its capacities. So when – in our parlance – the color or the smell
of the wax changes, the dog does not experience the successive colors or
smells as alterations in an enduring object, but perceives them in the
way in which we, human beings, might perceive (say) night following
day. Gassendi challenged Descartes on this score: "When a dog chases a
hare that is running away, and sees it first intact, then dead, and
afterwards skinned and chopped up, do you suppose that he does not
think it is the same hare?" (*Fifth Objections*: AT 7, 272–3; CSM 2, 190).
Descartes' curt reply was that he "observes no mind at all (*nullam
mentem*) in a dog" (AT 7, 359; CSM 2, 248). Why he observes no mind is
a question to which I shall turn soon; what matters for the moment is
that, in his reply, Descartes simply equates non-existence of mind with
the inability to see objects, even if the creature has eyes. It is not with
our eyes that we see wax or hares or people: something else is needed,

namely a mind – or, to use the word that Descartes himself uses at the end of our *Meditation* (AT 7, 34; CSM 2, 22), apparently as a synonym, an intellect (*intellectus*).

Nor is this all. Something further is involved in this mental or intellectual perception – something again of which the dog is bereft: Descartes calls it *judging*.

[F]

[In ordinary speech] we say that we see the wax itself if it is before us, not that we judge it to be there from its color or shape. . . . But then if I look out of the window and see men crossing the square, as I just happen to have done, I normally say that I see the men themselves, just as I say that I see the wax. Yet what do I see except hats and coats, which may conceal automata? I *judge* that they are men. And so something I thought I was seeing with my eyes is in fact grasped solely by the faculty of judgment that is in my mind. (AT 7, 32; CSM 2, 21)

I shall soon return to the automata wearing hats and coats, and look at them in their own right; for the moment, let us just take note of how they figure in the argument about judging. They come onto the scene, because they enable Descartes to make the point that we, human beings, live with the sense of possibly making a *mistake* in our perception: for all I know, the men I think I see in the square are mere automata; the wax, mere glue; the hare, a decoy. Now for us to have that sense, it must be that our perceptions already have a complex structure – *sentential*, in fact: were we to put in words what we experience as we perceive something, the words would make up a declarative sentence, for example, "there are men in the square," or "the wax smells of flowers." Why so? Because for a mistake to occur, a previously held belief (or *judgment*, as Descartes calls it) must turn out to be false, and beliefs require sentences to voice them. Animals, on the other hand, make no mistakes – because (Descartes *dixit*) they have no beliefs. A dog might of course pounce and break its teeth on a decoy hare; and we, spectators, might say that it has been fooled. But this is only a figure of speech: how can the dog have been fooled, how can it have misjudged, if it couldn't make a judgment in the first place?[11]

Now to the epilogue of the story.

[G]

I ask, what is the "I" that seems to perceive this wax so distinctly? Don't I know myself, not only much more truly and certainly, but also much more distinctly and evidently? . . . Whatever factor contributes to my perception of the wax or any other body, cannot but establish even better the nature of my own mind. (AT 7, 33; CSM 2, 22)

Descartes has just announced that he now perceives the wax much more distinctly than he did before; more distinctly, because he has clearer insight into the mental faculties involved in seeing it. Intellect, he has found, is involved – otherwise there would be no seeing *the* wax. And judgment is involved – otherwise there would be no chance of *mis-seeing* it. Still, as we read our text [G], we might want to ask: why do these insights bring Descartes greater knowledge of himself; and knowledge, to boot, that is "much more evident" (*multo evidenti[or]*) than his knowledge of the wax?

One possible answer is that Descartes now understands more clearly how his mind works. True. But it might also be that Descartes means something more radical: he might be saying that when he looks at the wax, he is bound to have also the idea of himself, looking. Granted, he does not say so outright; yet it is difficult to put another gloss on the sentences in the middle of our text [G]. I have left them out so far; here they are:

[H]
When I see, or think I see (I am no longer distinguishing the two), it is simply not possible that I who am now thinking should not be something. If I judge that the wax exists from the fact that I see it, it follows much more evidently that I myself also exist. . . . By the same token, if I judge that the wax exists from the fact that I touch it, the same follows – namely that I am. And if I so judge from the fact that I imagine the wax, or for some other reason, exactly the same thing follows.

No matter how Descartes comes to be aware of the wax – by sight or touch or imagination – this is accompanied by an awareness of himself. Thought always comes with the thought of oneself.

Still, what about his knowing himself "much more evidently" than the wax? Earlier in the *Meditation* (as we saw) this would have been asserted on the grounds that he could doubt that the wax existed while he could not doubt that he himself did. But these are not the grounds now: in the wax-discussion, the doubt has been suspended – Descartes is indulging common sense. So why does he know himself more evidently? Answer: because each of us knows his or her mind better than anything else. To each of us, his or her mind is transparent.

We have here the first glimpse of a doctrine that will loom large in Descartes' philosophy, and for which he is famous (or notorious). It only gets a brief mention in the present *Meditation* – the parenthesis on the first line of our text [H] where Descartes announces, as it were in passing, that he no longer distinguishes between his *seeing* and his *thinking* that he sees. Let me expand on that announcement, using a slightly different example. Suppose that during a class I turn to you and whisper,

"My, this is boring!" It would be very odd if you replied, "You are not really bored; you only think you are." Odd, because if I think I am bored, I *am* bored – period. The converse is also true. It would be equally strange if you declared afterward: "I may have been bored, but it didn't feel that way." Again, surely, if you didn't feel bored, you weren't bored – period. Such is the transparency of boredom: we cannot be *mistaken* about the occurrence of boredom in us, and we cannot be *ignorant* either. What is more, one might express that fact exactly the way Descartes does in the parenthesis of our text [H], and say that there is no need to distinguish between being bored and thinking that one is. The two go together.

Still, boredom is merely one case: are all mental states like that? Does Descartes believe they are? Does he think that there is no subliminal mind? It is part of the fickleness of the "piece of wax" that we get no definite answer to these questions. But then, this is only a first encounter; we shall meet the questions again, higher on the spiral, when the same expanses come again into view – that will be *Meditation Six*. Let us wait until then.

The time has come to glance back and take stock of where we are: what have we learnt about the human mind in the *Second Meditation*? I shall group matters under two headings, *thought* and *ego*. And I shall consider each of these via a contrast: Descartes' cast of mind somehow invites that approach.

Go back to the curt remark to Gassendi that he, Descartes, could not detect any mind in a dog. Ever since its first statement in the *Discourse*, this view has been a trademark of Cartesianism – remember the Port-Royal schoolchildren nailing dogs to planks and explaining that the cries of the dogs were only the noise of "small springs being deranged."[12] In a letter of 1639 (February 20: AT 2, 525; CSMK, 134), Descartes tells Mersenne that he has, in the past 11 years, spent much time on dissection; in fact, he doubts that any doctor has made as detailed observations as he himself has. He doesn't dwell on it, but odds are that many of these observations were on live animals. Question: did Descartes believe, like the schoolchildren, that he only heard the noise of small springs being deranged?

It is not easy to tell, for Descartes is cagey on the subject – even though other statements of his about connected issues are quite explicit. Yes, animals are automata (Part 5 of the *Discourse*: AT 6, 55; CSM 1, 139; and *passim*). Yes, they are like clocks (again Part 5: AT 6, 59; CSM 1, 141; also *letter* to Newcastle, November 23, 1646: AT 4, 575; CSMK, 304). No, they do not think at all (*letter* to Morus, February 5, 1649: AT 5, 278; CSMK 366). No, they have no minds (*Fifth Reply*: AT 7, 359; CSM 2, 248). Descartes usually points out that these yeses and noes are not downright certainties, only probabilities based on empirical evidence

– the strongest piece being that no animal speaks a language (again *Discourse*: AT 6, 56–7; CSM 1, 140; also *letter* to Morus: AT 5, 278; CSMK 366). But he is quite insistent that we wouldn't even think of wondering, were we not as adults still under the sway of prejudices inherited from childhood. In a vivid letter written in April or May 1638 (AT 2, 39–41; CSMK 99–100) he asks his correspondent Pollot to imagine growing up in an environment where there are no animals at all – only human beings and human-made automata. Well, upon encountering later in life his first animal, would it occur to him to doubt even for one instant that here was another automaton? Of course not.

So be it; but still, what does Descartes think about animals and *pain*? He has no qualms speaking about animals' "passions" – for example, the "fears, hopes and joys" of "dogs, horses and monkeys" (*letter* to Newcastle: AT 4, 574–5; CSMK, 303) – while in the same breath denying that these dogs, horses and monkeys have any mind or thought. Suppose, then, that a stone falls on my dog's paw and it starts moaning: might Descartes accept to speak of the dog's being in pain? Suppose he does; the question will be, what to make of the words. If you reflect, a spectrum of answers confronts us. At one end is the Port-Royal children's view: *pain* is just shorthand for a set of motions occurring in the automaton that the dog is, "springs being deranged" – think of dolls that wail when tilted. At the other end is a quite different gloss. Suppose that I – like Descartes – believe my dog to be devoid of thought. I cannot hold, then, that what goes on in him, as he wails, is an experience which, were it spoken, would be expressed by the words "my paw hurts." For one thing the words, put together, make up a sentence (or *judgment*, as Descartes would say) – something that a mindless creature cannot produce. Nor can such a creature say "paw": not having the idea of any objects, it has no use for nouns. Nor can it even say "my," since it has no sense of itself. There remains the final word, "hurts": must we erase it, too? Not necessarily – even if we call ourselves Cartesians. We *could* suppose that *some* experience is occurring in the dog, one that features no inner demarcation, no division between things in the world, no separation between the world and oneself, in fact no "oneself" – yet still an experience of kinds. If we want a name, we might call it *atmospheric*,[13] its content being just one vast, unstructured, all-encompassing datum. Sometimes it rains, and sometimes it hurts. Such will be pain, for my dog; and not just pain, but all the feelings that Descartes attributes to it and its congeners: fear, hope, joy, etc.

In truth of course, Descartes never speaks of "atmospheric" feelings, or anything resembling them. But the idiom is not incompatible with his thesis of animal unmindedness; and it has the merit of bringing out, by contrast, what the human condition is. A stone has fallen on my foot and I, too, groan. But *my* noise is a very different affair. It expresses a thought, for my sensation isn't just a sheer given: it has a structure, created by acts of the intellect. My big toe is what is hurting; perhaps it is broken; I am now asking questions, making judgments. Human feelings are for Descartes "thoughts" in this full-fledged sense, and not because of some honorific label affixed to them. As I hurt, I am "a mind, or intelligence, or intellect, or reason" – remember our line of text [B], early in the *Meditation*.

And as I hurt, I also have the thought of myself.

Descartes is almost certainly the first philosopher to have used "ego" not just as a pronoun, but as a noun also. This occurs early in *Meditation Two* – look to the *cogito* passage (AT 7, 25; CSM 2, 17; our text [A]). No sooner has Descartes uttered, "I am, I exist" than he extracts the pronoun, to remark that he does not yet understand well enough what "this 'I' " (*ego ille*) is.[14] The coining of the new noun is obviously not a mere piece of shorthand: it is meant to signal the existence of a certain entity – one that, it will turn out, displays remarkable features. The "I" is *omnipresent* to each of us, in the sense that its thought accompanies every thought that we have. And it is also *private*, in a special way.

The thesis of privacy is advanced in *Meditation Two* very much in Descartes' style – allusively. It receives no general account, only a passing mention via a brief example. Yet as we reflect on the example, we soon realize that it involves a deep, and controversial, vision of common humanity. Go back to our text [F] (AT 7, 32; CSM 2, 21), where Descartes criticizes ordinary ways of speaking. We commonly say that it is thanks to our eyes that we see the piece of wax; and in similar fashion:

> if I look out of the window and see men crossing the square, as I just happen to have done, I normally say that I see the men themselves, just as I say that I see the wax. Yet what do I see except hats and coats, which may conceal automata? I *judge* that they are men.

Let us take the fantasy about hats and coats seriously. Even if we close our ears to its schizophrenic undertones, we must surely wonder about the distance that it presumes to exist between, say, me and other human beings. Descartes is in effect saying that I have no direct and immediate certainty that there are other people – I know it only thanks to an inference, or a "judgment." There is a real gap between my assurance that *I* am an ego, and my assurance that *you* are. About me I know at once, as I sit in my study or look at a piece of wax. About you, I know it only thanks to a piece of evidence that you (fortunately?) provide: you utter words and sentences.

> None of our external actions can assure anyone who examines them that our body is not just a self-moving machine but also harbors a soul with

thoughts, except spoken words or other signs that have reference to particular topics, and have not to do with the passions.

This remark is not in a published text, but in a letter of November 23, 1646, to Newcastle (AT 4, 574; CSMK, 303), where Descartes also singles out speech – or rather its absence – as the decisive evidence that animals are just self-moving machines, or automata. So the ability to speak tells in both directions: if a creature has it, it is an "I"; if it has not, it is not. The speech need not be vocal, of course.

On the "hats-and-coats" view, then, your ego is something internal and private – in the sense that other people only ever see symptoms of it. If I say that *I* am bored, I speak of what I directly apprehend; but if I say that *you* are bored, I ascribe to you a state that I do not directly perceive, but of which I only discern outer marks – a slumping posture, or unfocused eyes, or yawns, or whatever. So strictly speaking, on this view, I never see you bored; I only see manifestations of your boredom. Likewise if you laugh at a joke, I merely gather that you have found it funny; and if a stone crushes your foot and you howl, I may see that your toes are bleeding but I do not see that you are in pain – I just infer that you are. And of course, things work in exactly the same way in the opposite direction: such is the distance between your ego and mine.

I want to end this perusal of *Meditation Two* with a reminder and a question.

Reminder. We are still early in the climb: perhaps as we move higher the view will change, the "I" will appear less internal and private, the divide between me and people in the square, narrower. Perhaps.

Question. Let us go back to *ego ille* – this "I" that Descartes has introduced us to. Surely we might wonder, why do we write here the word between quotation marks? or in italics? or use the Latin "*ego*" instead? The fact is, almost four centuries after the *Second Meditation*, we still feel uneasy about even how to set out typographically our translation of "*ego ille*."[15] De Luynes, the first translator (1647), decided not to render the substantivized pronoun at all: "*je ne connais pas encore assez clairement ce que je suis*" – "I do not yet know clearly enough what I am." Might his reluctance, might our typographical contortions, not be perhaps testimonies to the fact that this "I" to which we have just been introduced is a blurrier presence than the *Meditation* might lead us to believe? It might be useful to keep this question in mind, as we continue climbing.

me and my maker

Meditation Three is a long expanse – almost 20 Adam & Tannery pages, longer than all that has gone on before. Some of it is rugged terrain too, as Descartes appears to veer away from his resolve to avoid academic lingo, and has his argument rest on contrasts such as *formal* versus *material* falsehood, and *formal* versus *objective* reality – recondite idiom, to be sure. Nor is it just a matter of words. The aim of the *Meditation* is announced in the title, *Of God, that he exists*, so this will be a proof of the existence of God. Yet as we read, a worry intrudes: *a* proof? Soon after midpoint (AT 7, 45; CSM 2, 31) we are told that "from what has happened we must conclude that God necessarily exists," which would seem to close the matter. Yet somehow discussion goes on for another six pages, until we read (AT 7, 51; CSM 2, 35): "we must conclude . . . that it has been most clearly proved that God exists." Has there been a second proof, then? Or has Descartes simply been tying up ends left loose in the earlier proceedings? Whatever the answer, the progress seems less smooth than it had been in the earlier *Meditations* – which is not to say, however, that the guiding thought is ultimately opaque. In fact, the considerations to which Descartes appeals in proving that God exists and in describing what God is like, are not really all that remote, and as we shall see, they would have a special attraction to seventeenth-century readers. So – uncommon in Descartes – appearances in *Meditation Three* are more forbidding than reality.

A further preliminary remark. In seeking to prove the existence of God, Descartes stands of course in a long lineage of Christian philosophers, from St Augustine onward. But in the *Meditations*, the endeavor has a much more personal and dramatic tint. Don't forget: Descartes has supposed that a deceitful God might have rigged him to be like a clock that always told the wrong time. True, in *Meditation Two* he has discovered things that he could not be deceived about. But these certainties are few, and even *they* are in a sense precarious. When Descartes is actually immersed in the thought "I think therefore I am," he feels so convinced that he spontaneously exclaims (*sponte erump[it]*): "let whoever can deceive me, he will never bring it about that I am nothing so long as I continue to think I am something." But when he then turns to a different thought – namely, what a supreme deceiver could do – he can't help admitting that this deceiver could make him go wrong in every one of his beliefs, even those of which he is most certain. I have called this the *Adolf* predicament: someone at different, and specifiable by himself, times in the grip of opposite convictions – a disconcerting complex. There seems to be only one way to escape the swings of the pendulum: prove that God exists and that it is not possible that he be a deceiver – "otherwise I can be sure of nothing else" (AT 7, 36; CSM 2, 25). *Meditation Three* will be the first stage of the attempt; and early *Meditation Four*, the second.

But as Descartes starts on this stretch of the climb, a thought will surely cross the mind of the inquisitive spectator. If God really *does* deceive, could he not deceive Descartes precisely into believing that he (Descartes) had proved that he (God) did not deceive? Would that not be a very satisfying achievement for a supreme deceiver – if he happened to exist? So, as well as inspecting the steps of the proof that there is a God and he is no deceiver, we must watch how Descartes shields the proof, taken as a whole, from the ravages that the Deceiver might wreak on it, if he happened to exist. A double scrutiny awaits, then.

Let me begin with a personal tale. When my children were small, I made up a ditty to encourage them to eat their porridge at breakfast. How effective the words were is difficult to tell; but I was enormously proud of the tune to which they were set. It was witty, melodious, hummable – just charming. Yet along with the pride went a thread of unease: it was too good to be true! I could not really have composed that tune – it was above me; I must have heard it somewhere. Still, as no other source cropped up, I eventually came to accept authorship – until about 20 years later, when I heard the tune again: in a flute concerto of Mozart's. My suspicions had been right, after all.

Banal as it is, I hope my story has the merit of pointing to thoughts that are at the heart of Descartes' proof of the existence of God. For that proof will turn on the fact that he (Descartes) finds in himself one idea so exalted that he is sure he could not have originated it himself; it must have come from elsewhere. But where? It will turn out that as Mozart stands to me and the porridge melody, so God stands to Descartes and his exalted idea. It was God who put the idea into him; so God exists. We have yet of course to see what the exalted idea is, and attend in detail to Descartes' cogitations; but for the moment, and for the sake of simplicity, let me confine myself to drawing out some of the features of my involvement with Mozart.

Implicit in my doubts were at least four assumptions. The first was that melodies can somehow be *ranked* – ranked according to merit or perfection. There might not be any straight yardstick, it might be a pure matter of intuition; but there is rank nonetheless. I frequently listen on the radio to a program on which, if not the melodies themselves, at least their rendition is given a mark – "three stars," I hear, for example, to *this* recording of the *Hunt* Quartet. So it would not be out of place for me to believe that my porridge song featured, say, a five-star melody. A second assumption must also have been at work for my doubts about authorship to arise, namely that people, too, can be ranked – ranked with respect to the music that it is in their constitution to create. Some can only craft humdrum little tunes; others will compose haunting melodies. Call this a scale of native (musical) gift. And now we can enunciate the third assumption involved in my doubts – it would be some grand principle, such as this:

The more perfect the tune, the more gifted the composer.

Call this an axiom of fabrication. The final factor in my misgivings was a belief about myself – namely, that I was musically quite ungifted; so the odds were that I was not the maker of the tune. You might ask: why odds, and not outright certainty? The reason is that I might have under-estimated myself. Who knows, "perhaps I am something greater than I imagine and all [these] perfections . . . are somehow in me potentially, though not yet emerging or actualized." I have just quoted words from *Meditation Three* (AT 7, 46–7; CSM 2, 32).

If you reflect, though, these words can be uttered in opposite frames of mind – in my case it was hope; in Descartes', it is worry. *He* is looking for an idea that he could *not* have made up himself. Why? Because this would enable him to get beyond the stage he has reached in *Meditation Two*. Yes, he exists; but does anything else? Well, he can examine his ideas and

> if one of my ideas turns out to be [such] that . . . I myself cannot be its cause, it will necessarily follow that I am not alone in the world but another thing – which is the cause of that idea – also exists. On the other hand, if I find no such idea in me, I shall have no argument to assure me that anything exists other than myself. (AT 7, 42; CSM 2, 29)

The more Descartes can suppose an idea of his to be his own creation, the less reason he has to believe that something or someone else put it into him; the less reason to believe that he is not alone in the world. So authorship is something he wants to *dis*prove, at least in one instance; and much of *Meditation Three* will be the carrying out of such a dis-proof. Let us look at it, then, continuing to bear in mind my musical analogy.

First the matter of ranking – especially, ranking ideas. "Idea" is a word that Descartes uses liberally, and of which he often gives a definition. Here for instance is what he says to Hobbes: "I use the term *idea* to apply to what is established by reasoning, as well as anything else that is grasped [*percipitur*] in any way" (*Third Set* of *Replies*: AT 7, 185; CSM 2, 130). This is pretty broad: I can have the idea of a square tower, of a clock, of a tune, of a deceiving God, of the *cogito*. The question is, can these ideas be ranked? and how?

Here is one approach. Think of clocks – *they* can certainly be ranked, and not just for how accurately they tell the time but for other features as well. A clock usually shows hours and minutes, but this one might have a third hand, for seconds; it might ring – every hour, or every fifteen minutes, or even at whatever time we set it to; it might tell the day of the week, or of the month; it may need to be rewound only at distant time-intervals, or perhaps hardly ever; and so on and so forth. I have called all these things "features," a word that has the same Latin root as the one Descartes standardly uses in this context: for him, listed above are *perfectiones* of a clock (*perfections*, in French) – words that all come from *facere*, to make. Perfections, in this sense, have to do with the make-up of the clock; and still in this sense, we might say that a clock with more features is more perfect than a clock with fewer; or is more elaborate or more sophisticated – Descartes uses the word "*artificiosus*" (again, notice the root).

So much for clocks; turn now to the ideas of them. Might we not say quite naturally that the idea of a more elaborate clock has *more to it* than the idea of a less elaborate one – more thinking is involved? The idea of a clock, say, with three hands has more to it than the idea of a clock with two; and this is all the truer when the extra feature happens to be a novelty, and when having the idea involves the thought of how to fit the new feature into the overall mechanism. So, we seem to have found a simple way of putting *ideas* of clocks on a scale – it will simply be parallel with the scale of perfection of the clocks themselves. We might in fact use a single word, and say that just as clocks can be put on a scale of sophistication or elaborateness, so can the ideas of them. The more elaborate the clock, the more elaborate the idea of it.

Turn now to the owners of ideas – human beings:

If someone has the idea of a highly elaborate (*valde artificiosa*) machine, we are entitled to ask what caused it: has he perhaps seen such a machine somewhere, built by someone else? Or has he made such a thorough study of mechanics, or has he such powers of mind (*vis ingenii*) that he could think it up all by himself, never having seen it anywhere? All the elaborateness (*artificium*) present just objectively in the idea – the way it would be in an image – must be present in its cause, whatever that turns out to be.

This is from the *Principles*, the textbook intended for schools – Part 1, art. 17 (AT 8a, 11; CSM 1, 198–9).[1] "We are entitled to ask what caused it," says Descartes: why so? Presumably, it is because ideas are products and our old axiom of fabrication applies here, perhaps in this form:

The more sophisticated the idea, the more sophisticated its cause,[2]

and we want to find out what prompted the sophisticated idea: is it something that the person has actually seen, or expertise in the matter, or sheer "power of mind"? These were the relevant options when I wondered about the breakfast tune; and these are the options that Descartes will consider when he finds – not in another person, but in himself – one idea of supreme sophistication. The outcome will be a proof of the existence of God; let us look in detail.

One difficulty about the proof of *Meditation Three* is that Descartes, as he ranks his ideas, shuns for some reason the idiom of *artificium* (elaborateness) that he will use in the parallel text of the *Principles*, and resorts instead to the more academic-sounding jargon of "objective reality"; and in like fashion, instead of speaking of the *artificium* of what the idea is an idea of, he talks of its "formal reality." So for instance, in the jargon of the *Third Meditation* we should say that there is more *formal* reality in the three-handed clock than in the two-handed; and consequently, more *objective* reality in the idea of the three-handed clock than in the idea of the two-handed. As for the axiom of fabrication, it too is now formulated in terms of *reality*: "what is more perfect – that is, contains in itself more reality – cannot arise from what is less perfect" (AT 7, 40–1; CSM 2, 28); and even more scholastically, a few lines down: "for a given idea to contain such and such objective reality, it must surely derive it from a cause that has at least as much formal reality as the idea contains objective reality."

So be it; but we should remember that soon after this was written, Descartes switched to a simpler idiom for conducting the proof. Let me continue, then, to avail myself of the simpler, absent though it is from the *Meditation* itself.

We should also remember that Descartes is searching for an idea that is in him and yet is so elaborate, so sophisticated – *tantum artificiosa* – that he could not have framed it himself. As it turns out, he finds one – just one, but that is enough. His idea of *God*, as an "infinite, independent, supremely intelligent, supremely powerful substance" (AT 7, 45; CSM 2, 31), he could not have evolved alone: he lacks the mental power. What is more, there is only one way in which he could have acquired it: "God, in creating me, placed this idea into me – to be as it were the mark of the craftsman stamped upon his work" (AT 7, 51; CSM 2, 35). So God exists.

Obviously, for the proof to succeed, Descartes needs to show decisively that the idea of God is beyond his mental powers – beyond, in the way in which the tune of the porridge song was beyond my mental powers: I could carry it in my head, but had to have got it originally from somewhere else. What is it about the idea of God that makes it so sublime? Answer: it is the element of *infinity* or *supremeness* that it contains. When I think of God, I think of a being that is infinite, supremely (*summe*) wise, supremely powerful, etc., etc. – these qualities being not just potential, but fully present and actualized in him. Nothing in my daily experience enables me to frame *that* idea: in fact, it is only because I already have it that I see myself as finite and un-supreme in every way.

The thought that the idea of supremeness or perfection comes first, or is *innate* (AT 7, 51; CSM 2, 35), has of course a long history: Plato already voiced it in the *Phaedo*.[3] Attractive though it may be, it has nonetheless never succeeded in dismantling the opposite view – that, on the contrary, that idea is arrived at by abstracting from our own experience: we are conscious of our limitations and, as a result, imagine a being not subject to them. Nor are the few lines (AT 7, 45–46; CSM 2, 31) that Descartes devotes to refuting his opponent in any way decisive: he simply asserts that since there is more to the idea of an infinite being than to the idea of a finite one, that idea is "somehow prior" (*quodammodo prior*). One wonders: granted that there is more to a three-handed clock than to a two-handed, does it follow that the idea of the first is more innate than the idea of the second? And even if my idea of God *is* innate, why can only God have put it into me? I may innately distinguish black from white, yet hardly suppose that this ability has come to me from on high.

So in the end, the proof of God's existence really turns on the axiom of fabrication and the theory of rank that it involves – the view that a certain idea stands at the top of the scale, and can only come from a source that is at the top, too. Nor is it an accident that it should turn on this: the notion of scale, of rank, of degrees of *artificium*, would have immediate appeal to Descartes' readers, on a number of grounds. For one thing, it cohabits with machines – as we saw, that is how the proof is introduced in the *Principles*: the seventeenth century is when mechanical contraptions begin to count in people's lives and thoughts. And something else has begun to count, also relevant to the proof. Let me call it by its Latin name: *notæ*.

"Marks" – it is hard to think of them as novel. Yet such they were, more or less, when Descartes went to school at La Flèche: 1599 is the year when the definitive version of the *Ratio studiorum* came out – the manual of regulations that was to govern Jesuit pedagogy for the next 200 years; the manual, also, where the practice of assigning marks and grades to children was for the first time clearly laid out. There are to be class-lists; and in a list, the teacher will distinguish the largest possible number of grades [*gradus*] of students, namely: the best [*optimi*], the good [*boni*], the average [*mediocres*], the doubtful [*dubii*], those who must repeat the year [*retinendi*], those who are to be expelled [*rejiciendi*] – marks [*notæ*] that can be signified by the numbers 1, 2, 3, 4, 5, and 6.[4]

Note the injunction that teachers distinguish "the largest possible number of grades." Though the Jesuits did not literally invent grade and rank, they were the ones in Europe who made it an essential part of pedagogy – essential in the sense that from now on, grades were not just awarded as signs of merit or demerit, but became omnipresent factors in the educational system. Seats in the classroom were assigned according to rank, for example; and at the end of the year, the school honored publicly the students ranked highest. At the end of the year also, there were examinations to decide whether a student was to be promoted to the next class: dunces had to repeat the year. In one word – and I am using a word that, in European tongues, was also born in the seventeenth century – from now on students were to have a school *career*.[5]

In a later chapter I shall return to this development, and consider how it affected Descartes' thoughts on morality; for the moment I am concerned only with its link to *Meditation Three* – how it may have helped make Descartes' readers more receptive to the kind of proof that is there.

As can be seen from the samples of Jesuit class-lists that I append to this chapter (see below, pp. 63–70), one count on which students were graded and ranked was their intelligence, *ingenium*. The scale runs from "ultra-sharp" (*peracre*) to "blunt" (*obtusum*), with levels like "average" (*mediocre*) or "quite acute" (*acutum admodum*) in the middle – all these grades presumably reflecting similar grades assigned to the ideas that the students voiced in their written work or in class. For of course, our axiom of fabrication applies here: the more acute the work, the more acute the author. A teacher would not rank as *mediocris* a student who had voiced ultra-sharp thoughts in his essays and exams: he would not, unless – unless – he had reason to believe that these thoughts were not really the student's own! One striking fact about the seventeenth century is that, as school-marks become common, worry about academic dishonesty blossoms. The *Ratio* warns teachers against students who copy from their neighbor, or seek to leave the room during an exam (14: 5 & 14: 6, p. 147); or who commit fraud (*fraus*) in an essay (15: 13, p. 151). Even more explicit are the words of a pedagogic treatise written later in the century, also by a Jesuit father, de Jouvancy – the *De ratione discendi et docendi* (*On the Method of Learning and Teaching*):

> Least to be tolerated are those who do not so much write from themselves [*non scribunt de suo*] as stitch together bits from this one or that one [*ex aliis atque aliis consuunt*] – wretched interpolators [*interpolatores miseri*];

or even grow rich from literary thefts [*furtis litterariis ditescunt*] – infamous plagiarists [*infames plagiarii*]![6]

Incidentally, "plagiarism," "plagiarist," "*plagiat,*" "*plagiaire,*" are all words coined in the seventeenth century. Incidentally also, the *Ratio* strikes a blow for equality: it forbids teachers to plagiarize from their students (12–48, p. 146).

I have lingered on these developments – call them "the birth of marks," if you wish – because they very likely helped create a climate where the style of proof of *Meditation Three* would appear perfectly natural. Ranking one's ideas according to their sophistication? Descartes' readers would have been exposed to that from their first day in class. Wondering where an unusual idea came from? Concern about authorship would have been common currency at school. Granted, the coordinates in *Meditation Three* are more complicated. Descartes' idea of God comes not "from himself" (*de suo*: de Jouvancy's term), or "not from [him] alone" (*non a [se] ipso*: AT 7, 45; CSM 2, 31), roughly in the way in which we would say that a steroid-induced performance comes not from the athlete alone: ingestion of a foreign substance has enabled an accomplishment that is out of line with what the athlete would otherwise have achieved. Likewise for Descartes, it is as though he had imbibed a foreign chemical that now enables him to produce this remarkable mental performance – entertain the idea of God. Except, of course, that the image offered in the *Meditation* is not bio-chemical but techno-proprietary: the idea, we are told, is like "the mark of the craftsman stamped upon his work." Still, that image – too – carries the suggestion of a component distinct in kind from the rest of the works.

In the history of God's proofs, *Meditation Three* is not a significant event. No major thinker has, to my knowledge, trodden in Descartes' footsteps – no one has really believed that having the idea of God was such a feat of mental athletics. It does not follow, however, that the proof isn't interesting in other respects, for example in what it reveals about Descartes' picture of God and of human beings. Let me confine myself to a few short remarks.

First, a caveat. As he describes the idea he has of God, Descartes veers into deliberate paradox. On the one hand, God is the clearest and most distinct (*maxime clara et distincta*) of all his ideas; yet at the same time the idea is one that he does not grasp: "it is in the nature of the infinite not to be grasped by a finite being like myself" (AT 7, 46; CSM 2, 31–2). In setting up this contrast, Descartes relies heavily on the literal meanings of two verbs: *comprehendere* (= to grasp, to embrace, to put one's arms right around) versus *intelligere* (= to discern, to pick out).[7] When he thinks of God, everything he discerns is utterly clear and distinct; yet at no time can his mind encompass all that there is to God. Perhaps again, a musical analogy might help. Think of a memorable tune, say, the *Ode to Joy*. Once heard, never forgotten: the melody is utterly clear and haunting; simple, too – it involves just six notes on the scale. Yet together with this immediacy goes an aura of untold depths, a sense that no matter how often we sing or hear it, vistas will unfold, feelings will arise that we had not experienced on previous encounters. We shall never put our arms around it.

In God's case, this means that no matter what statement of Descartes' we fasten on, he can in fairness reply that it only expresses *one* perspective, *one* mode of seeing God's nature – no comprehensive view is attainable anyhow. With this escape in mind, let me turn to that final metaphor in the proof, the "mark of the craftsman."

A suggestive image, isn't it? Makers usually do aspire to have their name appear on their product. But more literally, the image also pinpoints the extent to which the *Meditations* offer a human-modeled picture of divinity. God is basically a craftsman – my craftsman. That image was already implicit in the supposition of *Meditation One* that God might be a deceiver: how would he deceive? By making me like a clock that always told the wrong time. It is explicit now, in the stamp-metaphor; and in the *Meditation* that is to follow, the *Fourth*, it will be omnipresent. For the problem that Descartes will seek to resolve is this: granted that God has not rigged me to be always mistaken, how is it that this superior *artifex* has nonetheless created such a faulty product – me, Descartes, prone to so many errors? And the solution will be that "no matter how skilled, a craftsman need not put into every one of his works all the perfections that he can put into some" (AT 7, 56; CSM 2, 39). All the key words are there, testimony to one fact: among seventeenth-century philosophers – perhaps among all philosophers – Descartes is the one who paints the most non-grandiose, non-transcendental, picture of God. To say *that*, is of course not to deny that there is another side, congruent with the doctrine of ungraspability: at various moments (we shall encounter some), Descartes will on the contrary insist on the infinitude of God, on the impossibility to understand God's nature – he refuses, on that ground, to engage in what he calls "theological" discussions. But these are only moments. Overall, and especially in the *Meditations*, Descartes' prose about God is very much in tune with the metaphor of the craftsman's stamp; in one word: prosaic.

We might also reflect on what the metaphor suggests about *us*, the products onto which the idea is stamped. The picture that emerges is very much one of mechanical contraptions into which their maker has, or has not, installed a certain fixture. It isn't just the metaphor itself, but the verbs that go with it – not only "stamp" (*imprimere*), but also "put" (*ponere*) and "insert" (*indere*). As we shall see, that trio of verbs will occur again, at the end of the *Fourth Meditation* (AT 7, 61; CSM 2, 42), when Descartes explains what perfections God could have put into him to make him less prone to making mistakes: again *imprimere, ponere, indere*. We should also take good notice of the fact that the fixtures that (we are told) have been, or could have been, imprinted or put or inserted into Descartes are all *mental* fixtures – ideas or mental faculties or mental capacities. Of course Descartes does not yet know that he has a body, so can speak only of his mind; but the fact remains, he often speaks of it in these simple, almost physical, terms. Maybe these are only images; maybe the view will change as we climb higher. But for what it's worth, that is the prose we confront right now.

As I have said before, *Meditation Three* is long and complicated. Even after God has been argued to exist on the basis of how sublime the idea of him is, more considerations are adduced – perhaps to shore up the argument, perhaps as a separate though allied proof. It's not easy to tell, and has been a matter of debate; I shall skip it. We should also remember that even if God has now been shown to exist, an important step remains: show that he does not deceive. That will occur at the beginning of *Meditation Four*;[8] I shall consider it soon.

For the moment, though, let me address another, broader, preliminary yet pressing, matter – how can Descartes deal with the charge that, given the hypothesis that God might deceive, the very idea of offering a proof that he doesn't is misguided? If God can fool you about anything, can he not fool you into believing that you have shown that he fools you about nothing? What would please a deceiver more? Descartes is seeking to prove that God is honest, yet it is only if God is honest that he can trust any proof; so he must assume the very thing he is arguing for. That was almost certainly the thrust of Hume's comment (I mentioned it in chapter 2, as we first encountered the doubt) that "Cartesian doubt, were it ever possible to be attained by any human creature . . . would be entirely incurable." Why incurable? because no medicine will work unless the patient is already cured. And it is also the thrust of a charge with which Descartes was confronted as soon as the *Meditations* appeared – brought by the second *objector*, Mersenne (AT 7, 124–5; CSM 2, 89); and again by the fourth, Arnauld (AT 7, 214; CSM 2, 150). Here is Arnauld:

> How does the author avoid committing a circle when he says that we are sure that what we clearly and distinctly perceive is true, only because God exists? Yet we can be sure that God exists only because we perceive this clearly and distinctly. So before we are sure that God exists, we need to be sure that whatever we perceive clearly and distinctly is true.

This has come to be called the *Cartesian circle*. A circle occurs when what one argues *for* is already assumed in what one argues *from* – for example when someone proclaims that God exists because the Bible tells him so, and then when asked why he trusts the Bible, replies: "because it is the word of God." Arnauld's charge is that, in proving the existence of God, Descartes relies on clear and distinct ideas, and yet when asked why he trusts *those*, his only reply is that God makes them reliable. Descartes took himself to have answered the charge; a sizable literature developed;[9] let me hazard a few words.

In his answer, Descartes asks us to reflect on the nature of *certainty*, on the thoughts and mental attitudes that go with it. Two words will turn out to be crucially important; but before we focus on them, it might help to glance back briefly to an earlier moment – the episodes of certainty and doubt that were canvassed in *Meditation One*.

Begin with the distant tower. As Descartes sights it from afar, it clearly looks round; but mindful of past experience, he is not on that account convinced that it *is* round: perhaps it is not. There is no certainty here, one way or the other. On the other hand, that feeling plainly colors the next episode – his sitting by the fire in his study: it is not so easy now to say "perhaps not." Descartes is nonetheless able to say it, for he can suppose that he is mad or dreaming. And he is likewise able to append the two words to his conviction that he has a body, or that he is not the only person in the world – God might be deceiving him on those scores.

Not all certainties, however, are like that.

If a conviction is so firm that we can never have cause to doubt what we are convinced of, there is nothing further to inquire: we have all that can rationally [*cum ratione*] be desired. What is it to us if someone should perhaps feign that that of whose truth we are so firmly convinced might appear false to God or to an angel, and is absolutely speaking false? What heed would we pay to this absolute falsity since we'd in no way believe in it, or have the slightest suspicion of it. For we have assumed a conviction so firm that nothing can remove it, and that conviction is clearly the same as the most perfect certainty [*perfectisssima certitudo*].

But it may be doubted whether any such certainty, any such firm and immutable conviction, is to be had.

. . .

Some [intellectual] perceptions are so clear and at the same time so simple that we can never think of them without believing them to be true; e.g. that while I think I exist, that what is once done cannot be undone, and similar truths about which we manifestly have this certainty. We cannot doubt them unless we think of them; but – as has just been said – we cannot think of them without at the same time believing they are true. Hence we cannot doubt them without at the same time believing them to be true; that is, we can never doubt them.

. . .

> Nor is it an objection that such truths might appear false to God or to an angel; for the evidence of our perception will not allow us to hear anyone who makes up this kind of story.

The text which I have just quoted at length is in the *Reply* to the *Second* set of *Objections* (AT 7, 145–6; CSM 2, 104); it is an answer to Mersenne, and Descartes will simply refer Arnauld back to it in addressing his charge of circularity. How it is meant to accomplish that task, I shall consider later; for the moment, let me confine myself to the matter of certainty.

The emphatic message is that some certainties cannot be directly doubted at all, not even via the supposition of a deceiving God. For when we are in their grip, we cannot even entertain that supposition: the "evidence of our perception will not allow us to listen to . . . that kind of story" (literally: "will not permit us to hear (*audiamus*) someone who feigns such things (*talia fingentem*"). Descartes gives examples: "I, while I think, exist" (the *cogito*); "what is once done cannot be undone," a logical truth; or (looking back to *Meditation Three*) "two plus three cannot be more or less than five," simple arithmetic. About all of these, we have "the most perfect certainty." Notice, incidentally, that as far as strength of assurance goes, the *cogito* is given no pride of place – it is one *perfectissima certitudo* among others.

Notice also that in paraphrasing Descartes I have added a word, one that he does *not* use: of these perfect certainties, I said that they were not *directly* doubtable. This is to make room for the situation that Descartes describes in late *Meditation One* and early *Meditation Three* – his ability nonetheless to tell himself, when he is not actually experiencing any particular perfect certainty, that perhaps God always deceives him, even when he feels perfectly certain. This is our pendulum swinging back and forth – "Adolf's predicament" I have called it, precisely what Descartes is now trying to escape.

Return to the *Reply*. As we see, Descartes affixes two adjectives to his perfect certainties: they are "firm" and they are "immutable." Just as a block of marble fills out entirely the space which it occupies, so a perfect certainty fills out entirely the mind which it inhabits: it will not allow that mind to "hear" contrary thoughts. That is firmness. Nor will the marble roll away; it will be there each time we visit the spot. Each time I shall be able to exclaim: "What does it matter if this appears false to God or an angel? I can't even entertain such a fiction." As well as being firm, my certainty is then also immutable.

These two features, however – firmness and immutability – are not bound to coexist: some certainties are firm today, but won't be tomorrow. Such is, of course, not the case with the ones mentioned so far – the *cogito*, for example, or "two plus three equals five"; but there are others. Imagine that you wonder whether the series of prime numbers is infinite, and are shown Euclid's elegant proof that it is.[10] You work your way through to its conclusion, and are at that moment as certain of it as of anything – though in this case, your certainty is not immediate like the *cogito*, but has been derived. It is as though you had started from a wonderfully lit front room,[11] and progressed along a corridor with opaque curtains drawn across it, pulling open one fold after the other so that the light now shines at the far end. The question is, will it continue to shine? Answer: only as long as none of the curtains you have pulled slides shut again. Even if you understood everything perfectly as you worked your way through the proof, a step or more may slip from your mind later on, and be gone: how many of us still remember the details of even simple mathematical proofs that we were taught at school? About the infinite number of primes? About the three angles of the triangle? The light of perfect certainty no longer shines at the end of *those* corridors; some of those firm teenage convictions have gone.

Let us return to God and the circle. Though he doesn't say so outright, it is clear that Descartes takes his *Meditation Three* demonstration of God's existence to be on the same intellectual level as, say, the proof about the three angles of the triangle: it is a deduction from self-evident premises. So if you attend all the steps, you are certain of the conclusion when you actually reach it. Once again you are able to exclaim: "What does it matter if . . . ? etc., etc." It is a firm certainty.

That rating was questioned by Descartes' interviewer Burman, in the *Conversation*, on the ground that it overestimated the powers of human attention: "our mind can think of only one thing at a time . . . and there are many thoughts that come to mind in a proof. So one will not be able to keep one's attention on all the axioms, for one thought will get in the way of another." We cannot keep all the curtains drawn open, as we trek along the corridor. Here is Descartes' reply:

> First, it is just not true that the mind can only think of one thing at a time. It is true that it cannot think of a large number of things at the same time, but it can still think of more than one. . . . Secondly, it is false that thought occurs instantaneously; for all my acts take time, and I can be said to be continuing and carrying on with the same thought during a period of time.
> . . . It is clear that we are able to grasp God's proof in its entirety; as long as we do this, we are certain of not being deceived, and so every difficulty is removed. (AT 5, 148–9; CSMK, 334–5)

Complex and long though it may be, the *Meditation Three* proof can still be compressed into a single thought; and so the certainty that graced the starting premise (say, the *cogito*) now also adorns the final conclusion (that God exists). As we entertain *it*, we cannot suppose that we might be mistaken. Illumination has come to the far room.

Still, you might wonder, don't we want something more, namely: that this conclusion should be *perfectly* – immutably – certain? We can imagine Adolf conducting a proof in his wife's arms and reaching the conclusion that she can, after all, be trusted in everything. Alas, his certainty never survives the cruel light of dawn. Similarly, will Monday's prover not have a relapse and tell himself on Tuesday: "Yes, I was sure yesterday that a truthful God existed, but how do I know that I was not being tricked yesterday by a deceiving God?" If this relapse can occur, Descartes has not escaped Adolf's sad fate.

Luckily, God's proof differs from every other proof. Your certainty about primes will fade when a step in the demonstration has gone from your mind; but no similar adversity can befall the conclusion of the proof of God's existence and trustworthiness. You may forget tomorrow one step or more of *Meditation Three* and early *Four*, but this will not in any way affect your assurance of the conclusion; the memory of having *once* been sure is enough. Light will continue to shine, even after a curtain has slid shut:

> [O]nce I have perceived that God exists . . . and is no deceiver . . . even if I am no longer attending to the arguments that led me to judge that this was true, as long as I remember that I clearly and distinctly perceived it, no counter-argument can be adduced to make me doubt it. (AT 7, 70; CSM 2, 48)[12]

So: once acquired, never lost. From now on, whenever Descartes thinks of God, he thinks of a necessarily honest maker; he realizes that "the faculty of intellect given to him by God cannot but tend toward the truth *(tend[ere] in verum)*" (AT 7, 146; CSM 2, 104); he can never again entertain the thought that he might have been so made as to be mistaken in what he most firmly believes; he can no longer *indirectly* doubt his perfect certainties; and if not indirectly, then not at all. He has escaped Adolf's fate.

The question is, has he escaped the circle? Has he met the charge that the very attempt to prove the trustworthiness of some of his certainties perforce assumes that some of them *are* trustworthy – those involved in the proof?

In one sense, Descartes can certainly answer that, no, he made no such assumption; he did not assume that his intellect "tended toward the truth" (I shall henceforth use this phrase as shorthand for what Descartes wishes to prove overall: the words are from the *Reply* – see the quotation a few lines ago). To make an assumption is to adopt, albeit sometimes unconsciously, a mental attitude where you shield yourself from entertaining doubts about what you assert. But, surely, no such shielding occurred in Descartes' proof of God; if anything, the opposite is true. Look back to the *Reply* (our long quotation on p. 58). Descartes imagines an inner voice interrupting, challenging, "what if this should appear false to God or to an angel?" Well, he could not even "hear" the interrupter. It is not that he was playing deaf; he was literally unable to entertain a certain thought. Of course once he has proved God's existence and integrity, Descartes has a reasoned assurance of his intellect's reliability; but that assurance was not already a factor in the proof as it progressed. So: no, he did not assume what he was arguing for; he did not go round in a circle.

True, true. Yet it is hard to escape the feeling that, somehow, there is more to the landscape than we have been given to contemplate – perhaps a subterranean rift. And a good way to probe might be to go back and look again at Descartes' plight at the beginning of *Meditation Three*, before the proof. Recall the peculiar mental conflict he recounts there: sometimes he cannot help thinking that he might always be deceived; at other times he is certain that he cannot there and then be deceived. It is precisely to put an end to these swings that he embarks on the proof that has just concluded. Well, let me ask a question that has to do with common psychology. Is it not likely that someone who experiences this sort of pendulum will, at times when he is reflecting and not in the midst of a swing, have an opinion about the relative rationality of his conflicting beliefs? Will he not be inclined to regard one of them as an affection, or affliction – a way in which he cannot help feeling in certain circumstances; and the other, as a belief that is intellectually respectable – arrived at, or buttressable, through reasons? Note that to view a belief of oneself as reputable is not the same as to hold it true: Adolf might take his despair about women to be rational, yet hope it mistaken. And conversely, he might regard his occasional inability to *dis*trust his wife as a sign of human weakness, yet hope it mirrors the truth.

What is Descartes' assessment of his conflicting beliefs as he sets out to resolve the clash between them? Which does he regard as an affliction – his doubts or his certainties? Reading the fine print would, I think, incline one to the second alternative:

> when I turn to the things themselves which I think I perceive very clearly, I am so convinced by them [*tam plane ab illis persuadeor*] that I burst out in these words [*ut sponte erumpam in has voces*]: "let whoever can deceive me, he will never bring it about that . . . two and three added together make more or less than five." (AT 7, 36; CSM 2, 25)

He "bursts out": this does sound like the report of an affection, of a way in which you can't help feeling in certain circumstances. Let me attribute to Descartes *that* assessment as he enters the proof – we shall soon see, there is in fact stronger evidence for that attribution.

Let me also engage in a flight of fancy. Imagine that a prescient (and not necessarily evil) genius should address our philosopher in these words: "You are in a state, Descartes, where your beliefs keep switching: at one moment you think that a wily God could deceive you about anything, while at the next you swear that about *this*, nobody could deceive you. Well, there is a train of reflection in which you can now engage, during which you will not be able to entertain the idea of God's deceit and will also view that inability as entirely rational. You will eventually become certain that God exists, is honest, has made your intellect so that it tends toward the truth; and these certainties will live on, so that never again will you worry about a deceitful God."

As is plain, this is a future-tense, second-person and condensed version of the *Reply* that Descartes offers to the charge of circularity. Tense and person have been changed so as to make the story more bi-personal – it is now advice given by an outside authority.

Why the fantasy? For one thing, it alerts us to the fact that Descartes' situation has parallels in other, more common, walks of life. Think of a young woman torn between conflicting thoughts about whether to put an end to a pregnancy that she has just discovered: might she not be told by a prescient giver of advice that if she opts for continuing, she will afterward be forever convinced that her choice was the right one? Again, we have inner conflict; again, the patient is advised to engage in a certain course – though this time, not merely one of cogitation; again peace of mind is the predicted outcome if that course is followed, peace achieved through inability, from now on, to believe in the other option, even fleetingly. What is more, that inability will be felt not as an emotional incapacity, but as the voice of reason: the rejected option will look plain wrong.

So much for the advice. The question is, what to think of it? The first point to note is that the recipient may well accept fully the prediction on which it is based. The young woman may well believe that, yes, once she has borne the child she will forever regard her decision as right. Similarly, Descartes may well believe that once he has gone through the proof, he won't ever again fret about a deceiving God. But somehow, that does not close the matter – if anything, it points to the problem. Don't forget that when he reflects on his conflict before engaging in the proof, Descartes (we saw) assigns his moments of certainty to the province of brute sentiment; and likewise, our young woman probably sees her desire to give birth as falling on the side of nature and instinct. Both are now told that perpetual peace will come to them, from *that* side – he will forever bask in his certainties, she will forever rejoice at having given birth. Might not this very promise induce a worry that the path they are about to follow is one where their critical faculty will have been, so to speak, tranquilized, so that they end up in what is really a Lethean sort of peace? Nor is the worry diminished by the assurance that this state will feel rational ("we have all that can rationally be desired," says the *Reply*): that might be the work of Lethe, too. Granted, neither Descartes nor the young woman has any strong ground for believing that this possibility is in fact the truth; but they have no ground for dismissing it either. So if they decide to follow the advice, and are not deliberately opting for Lethean beatitude, they are in effect tossing a coin. It is a leap of faith on their part.

Return to the circle. In one sense, Descartes' response to Mersenne and Arnauld is perfectly correct: what he has argued *for* – the reliability of his intellect – is not already assumed in any premise that he has argued *from*. So he has not walked in a circle. But there may still be something curious about the path that he has trod: it has brought him to a never-never-land. Never again will he worry about a deceiving God; never again will he think that perhaps his intellect does not "tend toward the truth"; and this peace of mind will come from the mere memory of having achieved a certain proof. So be it. But might Descartes not wonder whether perhaps that memory is sufficient only because the proof also carried some secret Lethean powers – it somehow brought oblivion of the doubts that prompted it in the first place. Remember Hume calling the doubt "incurable"? Well, it isn't clear that *Meditation Three* has shown him to be wrong. Presumably Hume had in mind only the intellectual import of demonstrations.

We shall meet the problem of incurability again, at a further bend of the road. But for the moment, let us follow Descartes' progress.

appendix

The grade sheets that follow are from Camille de Rochemonteix' study, *Un Collège de jésuites aux XVIIe & XVIIIe siècles: le Collège Henri IV de La Flèche*, 4 vols (Le Mans, 1889), vol. 4, pp. 348–50.

Rochemonteix gives no information about the date; but whatever it was, we can safely assume that Descartes' class would have been assessed in exactly this fashion. The translations are mine. As you can see, the grading is either numerical or by letter. The recorded assessments are, I hope, self-explanatory: d = *dubius* (dubious); me = *mediocris* (average); ma = *malus* (bad).

Perhaps the last three columns on the right, in the 5th and 3rd grade class-sheets, need some comment. Third from the end is the *class teacher's* final assessment of the student. But the Jesuits worried about possible bias; so at the end of the year, each student was examined by three *external* teachers, whose assessment is recorded in the penultimate column; and *that* ranking, if it differed from the actual teacher's, took precedence over it (see final column, for example, of François de La Marche, 3rd line in grade 5).

Incidentally, classes are named as they still are today in France: pupils entered school in grade 6 and made their way up to grade 1.

QUINTÆ 1 NOMINA	ætas	tempus scholæ	mores	soluta oratio	præcepta aut loca	ingenium	frequentia	judic. praecept	judici. exam.	ultima censura
Adrianus de St-Gilles	10	2 an.	bonus	1	1	ingeniosus puer	assiduus	A	AAA	A
Claudius de Foy	12	2 an.	minime malus	2	2	memoria valet	assiduus	A	AAA	A
Franciscus de la Marche	11	2 an.	bene moratus	2	2	ingenium minus promptum	abfuit aliquoties	D	AAA	A
Gabriel Dumesnil	11	2 an.	pius	1	1	ingenio acerrimo et memoria præstanti	assiduus	A	AAA	A
Guillelmus Avenel	13	3 an.	levis et dubiis moribus	3	3	vario et mutabili ingenio	abiit post tragædiam	0	000	0
Jacobus de Marguerie	10	2 an.	pius maxime ac diligens	1	1	acutum et subtile	assiduus	A	AAA	A
Johannes Le Fébure	11	3 an.	moribus diffido	3	0	hebes	assiduus sed minime diligens	M	MMM	M
Phillippus de Nôs	12	2 an.	versipellis et piger	0	3	ingenio mediocri	sæpius a schola abfuit	D	DDD	D

TERTIÆ 1 NOMINA	ætas et ingenium	tempus scholæ	mores et frequentia	soluta oratio	stricta oratio	græca	præcepta	judicium præcept.	judicium exam.	ultima censura
Johannes d'Herouville	14 an. ing. modico	3 an.	optimis moribus bene studet	me	me	me	modice eruditus	A	AAA	A
Johan. de la Porte	13 an. ing. acuto	2 an.	pius et assiduous	A	B	A	callet omnia commode	A	AAA	A
Josephus Saillanfest	16 an. ing. obtuso	4 an.	liberioris vitæ; sæpe abfuit	ma	ma	me	ferme omnino imperitus	M	MMD	M
Josephus de Launay	14 an. ing. peracri	3 an.	dubiis moribus diu ægrotavit	B	B	A	inter scholæ primos loca obtinuit	A	AAA	A
Ludov. De Bretteville	16 an. ing. mediocri	1 an.	bene moratus assidnus quod licuit per valetudinem	me	me	me	perparum eruditus	D	DDD	D
Mich. Robillard	15 an. ab ing. non bene constitutus	1 an.	pietæ inclytus et assiduus	me	me	ma	vulgo inter scholæ ultimos	M	MMM	M

FIFTH 1 NAMES	age	years at school	character	prose	rules, common-places	intelligence	attendance	teacher's assess.	examin. assess.	final grade
Adrien de St-Gilles	10	2	good	1	1	intelligent child	steady	A	AAA	A
Claude de Foy	12	2	not at all bad	2	2	good memory	steady	A	AAA	A
François de la Marche	11	2	good character	2	2	not very fast	sometimes absent	D	AAA	A
Gabriel Dumesnil	11	2	pious	1	1	very sharp; extraordinary memory	steady	A	AAA	A
Guillaume Avenel	13	3	unreliable and fickle	3	3	spotty and unsteady	left after the tragedy	0	000	0
Jacques de Marguerie	10	2	most pious and conscientious	1	1	sharp and subtle	steady	A	AAA	A
Jean Le Fébure	11	3	not to be trusted	3	0	dull	steady but very careless	M	MMM	M
Phillipe de Nôs	12	2	sly and irritating	0	3	average	often away from school	D	DDD	D

THIRD 1 NAMES	age and intelligence	years at school	character and attendance	prose	verse	greek	rules	teacher's assess.	examin. assess.	final grade
Jean d'Herouville	14 middling	3	excellent studied well	av.	av.	av.	middling knowledge	A	AAA	A
Jean de la Porte	13 sharp	2	pious and steady	A	B	A	easy mastery of everything	A	AAA	A
Joseph Saillanfest	16 dull	4	free-living, often absent	bad	bad	av.	ignorant in almost everything	M	MMD	M
Joseph de Launay	14 ultra-sharp	3	unreliable, often sick	B	B	A	among top rank at school	A	AAA	A
Louis. De Bretteville	16 average	1	good steady, so far as health permitted	av.	av.	av.	knows very little	D	DDD	D
Michel Robillard	15 has disability	1	remarkable piety; steady	av.	av.	bad	generally among last at school	M	MMM	M

LOGICORUM I NOMINA	INGENIUM	FREQUENTIA	MORES	ERUDITIO
Alexander de Villers	mediocri.	frequens.	bonis moribus.	mediocriter.
Armandus de Boishébert	satis acuto.	assiduus.	optimis.	bene.
Franciscus d'Agneaux	optimo.	assiduus.	pius admodum.	studuit.
Gaspard de Lesnaut	retuso.	saepe abfuit.	insignis nebulo.	nihil scit.
Guilelmus Le Vasseur R.C.2.	peracri.	assiduus.	insigni pietate.	notus omnibus.
Jacobus de Beauvais	ingenio deficitur.	saepius e schola abfuit.	impudens nebulo.	minime eruditus.
Johannes Le Vacher	ingenio non caret.	satis assiduus.	bene moratus.	satis studuit.
Joannes des Planches	ingenio modico.	in collegio frequentando assiduus.	minime malus.	infra mediocritatem.
Ludovicus de la Londe	acuto admodum.	diligentia singularis.	suavissimis moribus.	studuit optime.
Raphael Dubuisson R.S.F.	perspicacissimo.	in frequentandis scholis summa assiduitate.	ingenuus adolescens.	studuit diligentissime.
Simeon Le Tellier	ad logicam parum apto.	in schola assiduus.	gratus ac memor offic.	sat bene.
Stephanus Le Chapelain	ingenio ad summum mediocri.	satis assiduus.	modestus et charus omnibus.	parum eruditus.
Thomas de Blainville	minime acri.	propter valetudinem non raro abfuit.	a pristina bonitate non defecit.	multa nescit.

LOGIC I NAMES	INTELLIGENCE	ATTENDANCE	CHARACTER	KNOWLEDGE
Alexandre de Villers	average	regular	good	average
Armand de Boishébert	smart enough	steady	excellent	good
François d'Agneaux	excellent	steady	very pious	did study
Gaspard de Lesnaut	dim-witted	often absent	blatant idler	knows nothing
Guillaume Le Vasseur R.C.2.	very smart	steady	remarkably pious	knowledgeable in everything
Jacques de Beauvais	lacks intelligence	quite often absent	shameless idler	knows very little
Jean Le Vacher	not lacking in intelligence	steady enough	good-natured	studied well enough
Jean des Planches	modest intelligence	steady in attending school	not at all bad	below average
Louis de la Londe	totally smart	uniquely steady	most suave character	studied excellently
Raphael Dubuisson R.S.F.	most perspicacious	most steady in attendance	ingenuous adolescent	studied most diligently
Simon Le Tellier	no great gift for logic	steady	nice and conscientious	good enough
Etienne Le Chapelain	average, at best	steady enough	well-behaved	does not know very much
Thomas de Blainville	minimally smart	often absent for reasons of health	does not lack plain goodness	ignorant of many things

deception and rights

W e have yet to meet the proof that God is no deceiver – that he has not so made us as to be always mistaken. Here it is:

> It is impossible that God should ever deceive me; for in every fraud or deceit some form of imperfection is to be found; and although the ability to deceive may seem to be a mark of acumen or power, the will to deceive is undoubted evidence of malice or weakness. So it has no place in God.

This is AT 7, 53; CSM 2, 37: the first page of *Meditation Four*.[1]

What to say of these thoughts? Let us grant the case about malice: many lies indeed are self-serving or ill-intentioned – think of Iago; and we cannot credit (biblical) God with one of them. Ditto for weakness, if we mean by "weakness" the inability to achieve what we want by the means that we most want. Yes, lies and ruses are often prompted by impotence: would there have been a Trojan horse had the Achaeans been able to win in honest battle? Again, and again for obvious reasons, that brand of deceit cannot be attributed to God.

The problem with Descartes' argument is the central disjunction. We are told that "the will to deceive is undoubted evidence (*proculdubio testatur*) of malice or weakness": but is it beyond doubt that there are only these two possibilities? Take the matter of weakness. As we have seen,[2] Plato already insisted that gods had no need to deceive, and is quoted approvingly on that score by Descartes' contemporary Grotius. Yet it is difficult to escape the impression that this lineage of philosophic insistence exists largely because there are such strong forces ranged on the other side. Just think of how we speak. English (and not just English) is replete with words that have come to signify dissimulation, having begun life signifying power of some sort:[3] "crafty," "sly" (originally = "able to strike"), "artful," "cunning," "impose," "maneuver," "machination," "manipulate," "fabricate." Did they just change skin? Nor is it only words, but locutions also: "I've been had," "*je me suis fait posséder*," "he put one over on me." This vocabulary hardly suggests that we view dissemblers as weaklings (at least when we set them against their dupes). Nor is it just vocabulary, it is also our paragons – Ulysses for example. In Plato's dialogue *Hippias Minor*, Socrates asks Hippias who is better (*beltiôn*): Achilles or Ulysses? and proceeds to convince his incredulous respondent that it is Ulysses, because he at least knows the truth that he chooses to conceal (371e). "Better": is this mere Socratic irony? Not only the philosopher speaks in that voice, so does the poet. Homer, about Ulysses:

> . . . the grey-eyed goddess
> Athena smiled, and gave him a caress:
> . . .
> "Whoever gets around you must be sharp
> and guileful as a snake; even a god
> might bow to you in ways of dissimulation.
> You! You chameleon! Bottomless bag of tricks!"
> (*Odyssey*, book 13, 288–91)

Or closer to our time, and even closer to that of Descartes, we have Don Juan:[4] can anyone who has seen Molière's play or heard Mozart's opera believe even for an instant that Molière or Mozart regarded Don Juan as a puny figure, or punier for his deceits? "*Quel homme!*" exclaims the servant Sganarelle – ambiguously of course, but – ambiguously. True enough, Descartes will try to make room in his argument for the aura surrounding these "Olympic" liars, by contrasting ability and will: Don Juan may have been able to make 1,003 Spanish ladies believe that he loved them, but he still is a weak man – for having wanted to do it! Well, perhaps. Yet Descartes ought to be a little more loquacious in describing that weakness, especially in view of the fact that he writes at the exact time when in Europe the conceptual ties between power and *untruth* are about to grow stronger. Why this is about to happen, we shall see very soon; for the moment let us take a brief look at the other pole of Descartes' disjunction, malice.

Yes, there are Iagos. But are there not also Marlows – the stranger in *Heart of Darkness* who tells Kurtz's abandoned fiancée that the last word Kurtz pronounced was her name? Surely, people often utter *good* lies, i.e. lies that aim to improve the life of the person to whom they are told. Imagine for example that the universe consists of colorless, odorless, and soundless atoms; but God has so made us that we see sunsets, smell roses, and hear trilling birds. Wouldn't that be deception – for our benefit? This is exactly the question that Mersenne asked in the *Second* set of *Objections*:

Cannot God treat men as a doctor treats the sick, or a father his children? In both these cases there is frequent deception though it is always employed beneficially and with wisdom. For if God were to show us the pure truth, what eye, what mental vision, could endure it? (AT 7, 126; CSM 2, 90 – note the last sentence)

The same question, with the same paradigms of good lying, was raised by Hobbes, the third *Objector*:

The standard view is that doctors are not at fault when they deceive their patients for their health's sake, and fathers are not at fault when they deceive their children for their own good. . . . M. Descartes ought therefore to consider whether the proposition "God can in no case deceive us" is universally true. (AT 7, 195; CSM 2, 136)

Descartes' answer is puzzling. He has no wish, he says (AT 7, 143; CSM 2, 102), to deny that God "may through the prophets engage in some verbal lying, such as doctors engage in when they deceive the sick so as to cure them"; however, in the *Meditations* he had in mind "not lying as it is expressed in words, but the internal and formal malice inherent in deception." This seems to weave together two quite different distinctions, that between verbal and non-verbal, and that between malevolent and non-malevolent. True enough, God as imagined in *Meditation One* would deceive not by lying but by rigging (as I have called it) – not by whispering falsehoods into my ears, but by so creating me that I harbor only false beliefs. It is hard to see, though, how that divide has any relevance to the question that Mersenne and Hobbes asked: might not fathers rig matters as well as tell lies – stage Santa Claus, for example? If, on the other hand, Descartes is basically contrasting malevolence with non-malevolence, and saying that in the *Meditations* he had only malevolence in mind, because non-malevolent deceit isn't really deceit: if *that* is his stance, then he is surely conceding too much. Go back to the sentence in *Meditation One* that started it all: "How do I know that God has not so created me that I be always mistaken?" Does the reply to Mersenne mean that Descartes worried only about being *deceived* by God, since this would imply malice, and did not mind being so made by God as to be forever *mistaken* – provided he were to benefit, as patients do from the lies of their doctors? Are we to understand that he was prepared all along to allow *that* possibility? This would make his doubt considerably less searing – less "hyperbolic" – than we have been given to believe.

Let us assume, then, that Descartes does not mean seriously his answer to Mersenne. Even so, it is significant that he should give it; for it almost certainly reflects the fact that, as he writes, a change has occurred in European thoughts about deception. The idea that benevolent deceit is not really deceit is now more apt to elicit ready acceptance – because it can now receive a ready justification. It is time that we looked at the new landscape.

Shakespeare's Iago tells his lies in order to have a rival officer dismissed, perhaps even put to death; Molière's Tartuffe tells his so as to rob a naive benefactor of his estate: here, then, are two instances of lying, with two different aims, each of them evil. Well, some moralists have held that when we disapprove of lies and deceits, it can only be for the particular harm that each of them brings about or aims to bring about – if indeed it does. Here, for example, is Hobbes, in his *Objection* to Descartes (AT 7, 195; CSM 2, 136: this is the sentence I omitted when I quoted from this source above): "the crime of deception resides not in the falsity of what is said, but in the harm done by the deceiver" – where, by "harm," he manifestly means the harm specific to each occurrence of deceit. In my examples, it is loss of life in one case and loss of property in the other. Most moralists, however, have dissented from this Hobbesian, call it "particularist," outlook; and held that over and above the specific harms that individual lies cause or aim to cause, there is a generic harm common to all lying, to all deceit. The problem is to say exactly what it is.

As it happens, for centuries (millennia?) an answer has existed, according to which lying is wrong – is a sin – in that it *corrupts the soul* of the liar. Perhaps the philosopher who asserted this most forcefully was St Augustine: here for example is a text (*De mendacio*, sect. 3, §10; p. 268) where he discusses the well-known conundrum: what if telling the truth should result in your own death?

> Even as we seek to preserve our body, we must avoid corrupting our soul through a lie. . . . Since no one doubts that the soul is superior to the body, over and above the integrity of our body we must put the wholeness of our soul – which can endure forever. But who would dare call *whole* the soul of a liar?

People might of course disagree with Augustine's rigoristic stance; but the idiom, the language of "wholeness of the soul," is what everyone in Europe would have used until the late 1500s.[5] Matters were about to change, however, drastically.

Here is a text written not long before the *Meditations*:

> Of lying, insofar as it is forbidden by its very nature . . . no other account can be given than this: it is the violation of a standing right of the person to whom discourse or signs are addressed. . . . The right in question is not general or derived, but specific to this form of exchange and born with it. It is none other than the freedom of judgement that human beings are understood by a kind of tacit agreement to owe one another in their verbal intercourse.

This is Grotius' *De jure belli ac pacis* (3.1.11), published in 1625.[6] Three things jump out, even in the first sentence. First, the announcement that we are to be offered an anti-Hobbesian, "essentialist," account: we are to be told why lying is forbidden "by its very nature." Equally striking are the words that come next: "it seems that no other account can be given than this." No other account: really? As we have seen, a canon about the wrongness of lies has been in place for centuries, St Augustine's, quite different from the story that we are about to hear. So the lead-up in that first sentence can only be seen as a manifesto: old, outworn, ideas are being cast out. And finally comes what we are being led up to – the proclamation of what makes lying "by its very nature" impermissible. Liars, we are told, violate a standing right of those to whom they speak, the right to freedom of judgment.

The thought just voiced may look commonplace to us now, but at the turn of the 1600s it was not. For the vision of human beings as bearers of rights or entitlements against fellow-humans or against authority was born in Europe around that time; or born at any rate then, the idiom that expresses this vision – an idiom that we still use. Grotius' *De jure belli ac pacis* is probably the first document where it flourishes: one might almost view that thick tome as a long catalogue of the *jura*, or "rights," that individuals possess in war or in peace. For example, if you are my neighbor and have already lit a fire, I have the *jus* to take a burning twig from your fire in order to light my own (2.2.11); or draw water to drink from the brook that runs through your land, if no brook runs through mine (2.2.12); or the right to have my slaves and mules returned to me after the war, if they had been taken away during it (3.9.3). Some *jura* are of course more abstract, as for instance the one we are considering right now in connection with Descartes' deceiving God – the right to freedom of judgment.

We shall need to ask what this freedom of judgment is, a freedom that is injured when a person is told a lie or is deceived in some other manner: I leave discussion of this topic till the final chapter. For the moment, let us take notice of a more general matter. Look back to the Augustinian explanation of the wrongness of lying, and compare it to the one offered in our Grotean paragraph. There is almost an ocean between the two. The older view located the wrong of lying in something that befell the liar – his heart was being destroyed, his soul was being corrupted: call this an *internalist* view. By contrast, the new account locates that wrong in what happens to the intended dupe – his or her freedom of judgment is being violated: call this, by contrast, an *externalist* explanation. It is as though the harm inherent to lies and deceit had emigrated from the deceiver to the dupe.

Of course, it isn't just in thoughts about *deceit* that this emigration will have occurred. Odds are that it took place on a wider front – and Descartes can hardly have remained immune; and so let us look at how thoughts of rights come into the *Meditations*, starting with the topic that has preoccupied us of late: deceit, and more particularly God's deceit.

Though they are nowhere mentioned, rights are almost certainly the pedestal of Descartes' answer to Mersenne – the pedestal of the view that benevolent deceit isn't really deceit. How so?

Let us think of rights in general. As we know, they have their vicissitudes: a right presumed to exist may in fact not exist; or it "may have existed but be now obsolete, thanks to the rise of another, supervening, right" (*De jure*, also 3.1.11); or it may have been forfeited; or it may have been renounced, explicitly or tacitly. Here is what Grotius says about benevolent lying (3.1.14):

> [W]henever it is clear that a recipient of discourse will not resent the injury to his freedom of judgement, but will in fact welcome it because of some good it brings him, then you have not committed a lie in the strict sense (i.e. an injurious lie); just as you would not commit a theft if, presuming the owner's consent, you were to use a small possession of his to secure him a great benefit. For where there is clear certainty, a presumption is taken for express consent; and no one is injured who consents.

When a doctor tells an untruth to her patient for the sake of his health, she is telling him no lie in the strict sense of the word – for she can assume that he has on this occasion *tacitly renounced* his right to freedom of judgment. Truth, therefore, is not owed to him; no right of his is violated; no lie has been spoken. This may look like a simplistic and grossly permissive view, in that it absolves the doctor of all misgivings; yet it remained the common currency on the subject in Europe for almost two centuries.[7] Jean-Jacques Rousseau put it like this in his fourth *Promenade*: "If you give counterfeit money to someone to whom you owe nothing, you may be fooling that person, but you are not robbing him."[8] Rewording Descartes' reply to Mersenne in terms of Rousseau's quip, we might say that if God makes us believe there are roses and sunsets and singing birds when there are only atoms, he might be giving us counterfeit money; but he is not robbing us, he is not *deceiving* us in any way.

As it happens, some objectors to Descartes were to push this line even further:

> [M]ay not God delude us continually by sending semblances or ideas into our souls? . . . God might do this without injury or injustice, *and we would have no cause to complain of him*, since he is the supreme Lord of all things and may dispose absolutely of his possessions.

These are the *Sixth Objectors* (AT 7, 415; CSM 2, 280). The tell-tale words are *absque injuria & iniquitate*, "without injury or injustice": we are hearing the voice of the rights-theorist, a voice that rings even clearer in the French translation (AT 9a, 220). For there, after the mention of what God could do without injury or injustice, Clerselier (the translator) inserts the clause I have italicized, "*nous n'aurions aucun sujet de nous plaindre de lui*"; and for good measure a few lines later, after the reference to God's absolute dominion, he adds the canonical word itself, "*il semble avoir le droit de le faire*": "he has, it seems, the right to do it." God has the right, of course – because against him, we have none.

We have just encountered a tricky question, one with which the seventeenth century will cope diversely. Go back to the *De jure*. In its opening pages, after having remarked that people use the word "*jus*" to mean all sorts of things, Grotius announces that he will employ it "in a strict and proper sense" – to denote a "*creditum, cui ex adverso responded debitum*": a "credit, to which a debt corresponds on the opposite side" (1.1.5). Defined in this way, rights are basically adversarial powers; they are held *against* someone. My right to a burning twig, for example, is against my neighbor; he, in this situation, has a debt toward me: he owes me a twig. Well, suppose that you view rights in this Grotean manner, as indeed we still do (at least some of them – we call them "claim-rights"); the question will arise, have we any rights against . . . God?

Some seventeenth-century philosophers do not see this as a problem. Leibniz, for example, will write in the *Monadology* (article 51) that "a monad demands with good reason [*demande avec raison*] that God in setting up all the other monads from the beginning of things should take it into consideration" – "*demande*" is standard rights-lingo. And three articles later: "each possible [world] has the right to claim existence [*a le droit de prétendre à l'existence*] according to the perfection that it involves." So, pre-established harmony and the best possible world are rights of the monads against God – Leibniz does not even bother to offer a justification, he just declares.

Many seventeenth-century thinkers, however, stand on the opposite shore – as do, for instance, the *Objectors* whom I quoted a page ago. God cannot be supposed to have obligations toward human beings. So if God were to "send continual semblances to our souls," even non-benevolent ones; if for instance he were to make us perceive just atoms where there were in fact sunsets, flowers and birds; even if he were to do *that*, he would be doing it "without injury or injustice." Why? Because there are no rights for him to injure; and consequently, no deceit on his part.

The *Sixth Objectors* were not alone in holding this view. It had already been voiced by Grotius in the *De jure* (3.1.15): "God has a supreme right over human beings" – supreme-*jus* on one side of course means zero-*jus* on the other. And it will be voiced even more vividly a few decades later, in 1696, in a well-known compendium of contemporary discussions: Pierre Bayle's *Dictionnaire historique et critique*. Bayle is writing about skepticism:

> [T]he more you raise the rights of God to the privilege of acting contrary to our ideas, the more you destroy the only means left to you to prove that there are bodies – namely that God does not deceive us and that he would be doing so if the corporeal world did not exist: to present to people [as real] something that does not exist outside their own minds would be deceitful.
>
> For [the skeptic] will answer, *distinguo* – "I distinguish": if a prince did so, *concedo* – "I grant it"; if God did so, *nego* – "I deny it": for the rights of God are quite different from the rights of kings.[9]

The skeptic's thrust is plain enough: unlike kings, God has no obligation toward his subjects; ergo, they have no rights against him; ergo, if he makes them believe massive untruths, even non-benevolent, he will not be violating any right of theirs; he will not be deceiving them. Absolute power is in no way wedded to truth.

Let me return to Descartes: he would know well enough what his objectors have in mind when they insist that God could make us continually take semblances for truths – "without injury or injustice." Yet once again his reply is evasive. Instead of confronting the charge, he resorts to what looks like a totally new line of defense: "[I]t is contradictory that human beings should be deceived by God: this follows clearly from the fact that the form of deceit is non-being, toward which the supreme being cannot tend" (AT 7, 428; CSM 2, 289). And he goes on at once to discuss other matters, scriptural – how to construe sayings of Saint Paul and King Solomon that the objectors had adduced in support of their challenge. Nor do I know of any passage where Descartes explains the thought voiced so pithily here. "Tend toward nothing" does recur as a tag on deceivers in 1648, in the *Conversation* with Burman (AT 5, 147; CSMK, 334); and again a year later (April 23, 1649) in a *letter* to Clerselier (AT 5, 357; CSMK, 378), but again unglossed both times, and bare – except for the comment to Burman that this is a "metaphysical consideration, perfectly clear to all those who give their mind to it."

So what are we to say, in the end, about Descartes' proof that God does not deceive?

First we ought to remember that the proof is not a minor hurdle in Descartes' path; he needs to clear it so as to dispose of the doubt. Also, the proof turns on questions that are of perennial interest and that intrigued the seventeenth century – exactly what is deceit? When do we commit it? Why do we disapprove of deceivers? Why do we deride gullible dupes? Why do we dislike compulsive tellers of truth? etc., etc. Given the richness of the subject, one can only regret that Descartes should have treated it as airily and evasively as he does. As we saw, in the *Meditation* he rests his case on a blunt disjunction: deceivers are either malicious or weak, and God of course is neither. When challenged about the first disjunct (by Mersenne and Hobbes), he equivocates; and when challenged about the second (by the *Sixth Objectors*), he simply ignores the question and turns to a new argument, again presented ultra-briskly: deceivers tend toward non-being, which it is impossible that God should do.

So let me end with two conjectures. Even though he will offer once again after the *Meditations*, and just as airily, the malice-or-weakness argument – in *Principles*, Part 1, art. 29 – odds are that, if challenged again, Descartes would fall back onto the "metaphysical" line, the one about deceivers "carrying themselves" (*feri*) or "tending" (*tendere*) toward non-being. After all, *that* is his final word, if we look at the entire corpus; and beyond its intuitive appeal, it has the merit of resting on notions that are sufficiently abstract and internalist-looking to discourage a challenge based on rights. Why should Descartes want to thwart such a challenge? Why is he evasive when confronted? The reason (and here is my second guess) is that on the matter of rights in general – and even more, of rights against God – Descartes has a Janus-like posture: officially an adherent of Grotean orthodoxy, he nonetheless feels strong attraction toward Leibniz-type egalitarianism. We shall see these contrary forces at work clearly enough as we turn to the main topic of *Meditation Four* – human error.

The topic arises quite naturally. Descartes has just found that he need not worry about being *always* mistaken; but he still has to live with the disagreeable fact that he is so *frequently* mistaken. "I am prone to countless errors" (AT 7, 54; CSM 2, 38). How is that so? And why is that so?

It is useful to separate these two questions – an example might help. I have just brought my bicycle home from its spring tune-up, and notice that the front wheel does not revolve quite as it should: at one point in each rotation, the rim rubs, however slightly, against the brake-pad. The wheel is probably a little bent: not all its circumference is on a plane perpendicular to the axle. So now I have an explanation of *how* it is that the rotation isn't quite right – a diagnosis, we might say, of what is amiss. Yet that is not the end of my questions. I might also ask myself, perhaps with a sense of surprise or even irritation, *why* is that defect there, why did the mechanic not correct it? did he perhaps even create it through repairing other fixtures – perhaps he tightened the brakes too close, for the sake of safety? This is a different order of questioning: it has to do with the history of how the diagnosed defect came about, or was allowed to remain. So we should distinguish between what one might call plain *diagnosis* – understanding where the trouble is – and, on the other hand, *case-history* – being able to tell how the trouble has arisen or has not been corrected. Of course there isn't always a clear dividing line between the two domains: history and diagnosis interact. But in a rough way at least, the distinction can be made; and it will be helpful to keep it in mind as we study the account of human error that Descartes offers in *Meditation Four*. In fact, I shall if anything exaggerate it – looking at what I call "case-history" in the next few pages, and leaving the matter of diagnosis until the chapter that comes after.

There is of course one clear difference between Descartes' predicament and the problem with my bicycle: the contrivance whose malfunction he is trying to explain is himself. So this will be, on his part, an exercise in self-examination. But there are also similarities, including one that I have not labored so far, and which yet deserves to be stressed.

One striking fact about *Meditation Four* – concealed somewhat in its translations – is how often words occur in it that have to do with *debt*. The verb itself, "*debere,*" appears nine times; the noun or adjective designating my condition when I am not given what is owed to me, "*privatio*" or "*privatus,*" eight times. Other members of the family are there too, not very distant cousins – we have met them recently, and will meet them again. For the moment, though, let me confine my attention to the two that I have just mentioned.

How does the idiom of *debere* come into the meditation? Descartes, as we saw, notes that he is prone to countless mistakes, and his first reaction is to ascribe the proneness simply to his limited faculties: the power that God has given him to discern true from false "is not infinite" (AT 7, 54; CSM 2, 38). God has not given him the power to discern red from infrared, either (my example). Yet almost at once, Descartes repudiates this first reaction – "this is not entirely satisfactory"; and he repudiates it by appealing to the notion of what is *owed* to him. When he errs, he is victim of a *privatio*, he "lacks some knowledge that somehow ought to [*deberet*] be in [him]" (AT 7, 55; CSM 2, 38). And he continues: "[W]hen I consider the nature of God, it does not seem possible that he should have put into me a faculty that is not perfect of its kind, i.e. is deprived [*privata*] of some perfection that is owed [*debita*] to it."

"*Privata–debita*": it is within the framework of this coupling – and of the question it enables to ask: "How can I be deprived of what I am owed?" – that *Meditation Four* will unfold.

You might wonder what entitles Descartes to suppose that when he makes a mistake, he has been deprived – a debt toward him has remained unpaid? There is no privation, for example, in my not distinguishing red from infrared. On the other hand there would be, if I were unable to distinguish red from green; and even more – this is the standard example from the Schools – if I were blind. Why so? Because sight, and the ability to distinguish the main hues of the spectrum, are the normal faculties of members of my species. Well, suppose that, in my head, I multiply 13 by 17 and come out with the wrong result: why should this be equated with my being unable to tell red from green, rather than equated with my being unable to tell red from infrared? Why is it not a mere limitation, but something worse – a privation? Was infallibility owed to me?

Yes, Descartes will reply; and the reason has to do with who my maker is. Look back to the passage I quoted two paragraphs ago: "when I consider the nature of God, it does not seem possible . . ." Why does it not seem possible that I should have a defective faculty of multiplying? Answer: because my maker is God, a supremely skilled craftsman; and

The more skilled the craftsman, the more perfect the works that come from him. (AT 7, 55; CSM 2, 38)

We are meeting again an axiom of fabrication – in fact the converse of the one that Descartes appealed to in *Meditation One*. There, you may remember, he used the dictum

the less skilled the craftsman, the less perfect the works that come from him

to argue that the atheist had even more reason to doubt his faculties, more reason to suppose he might be mistaken even where he was most certain – he was, after all, the product of random causes. Now, after *Meditation Three*, Descartes' condition is of course reverse to that of the atheist: he *knows* that he is an opus crafted by that incomparable craftsman, God. So now the reverse axiom applies: why does he, Descartes, make any mistake at all? Nor, if you reflect, is the axiom very far removed from my bicycle story: I brought the mount to a professional caretaker, so why does a wheel rub against the frame? Here again is a *privatio*.

So much for *privatum–debitum*. Unsurprisingly, the seventeenth century will add a further word to that coupling: to be deprived of one's due will now be seen as being deprived of something to which one has a *right* – this is our Grotean equation. Also: if one is so deprived, one has a right to *complain*. Well, again unsurprisingly, this forensic vocabulary is ultra-present in *Meditation Four*. Descartes will consider at length (AT 7, 60–1; CSM 2, 42–3) whether he "should complain" (*debere queri*), whether he has "cause to complain" (*causam conquerendi*); and will eventually conclude that no, he has "no right to complain" (*nullum jus conquerendi*). Why he has not, we shall see shortly; what matters for the moment is that we take good notice of the courtroom tonality of all these concerns – all the more because it creates a quandary for Descartes' readers.

Ask yourself, who would have been defendant in the suit had Descartes decided that, yes, he had a right to complain? It would of course have been the craftsman who had assembled him in the first place, namely God; which brings us once again to the vexed question: do human beings have any rights against their maker?

As straight words go, Descartes' answer is quite categorical. In the midst of discussing his privations, he at one point (AT 7, 60; CSM 2, 42) interjects that God "has never owed me anything" – *mihi nunquam quicquam debuit*. The message is plain: no debt on one side, no right on the other. Descartes has no rights against God. Yet it is hard to resist the impression that somehow Descartes' attitude is more complicated; that he is not really such a strict adherent of Grotean orthodoxy; that he is perhaps even confused about the matter. After all, if he held without further ado that God owed him nothing, would he not dismiss the very idea of complaining about the make-up that God has given him, as downright absurd? Yet nowhere in *Meditation Four* does this happen. Descartes will spend page after page showing that, although his mistakes are innumerable, he has no cause to complain about his maker. Mistakes are erroneous judgments; and judgments (so he tells us – I shall discuss the doctrine in the next chapter) involve the intercourse of two faculties, intellect and will. Well, might one of these be defective? No, each of them is "perfect of its kind" (*in suo genere perfecta*) (AT 7, 58; CSM 2, 40). However, one "extends further" than the other (again, to be explained in the next chapter); and mistakes arise from that disparity. Well, couldn't God have put into Descartes some mechanism to counter the imbalance – for example have "impressed on [his] memory that [he] should never make a judgement when [he] does not grasp clearly and distinctly" (AT 7, 61; CSM 2, 42)? Yes, he could have. And so we reach the final verdict: if God had made him that way, Descartes would be a more perfect creature – considered as a separate unit. But the world as a whole would be less perfect. For there is more perfection where creatures are not all exactly alike, even if this means that some are not immune to error (AT 7, 61; CSM 2, 43).

Whatever we think of the merits of this argument, much more noteworthy is the fact that it should be offered at all; it tells something about Descartes. Surely if he believed wholeheartedly that God "owed him nothing," the very thought of an apologia for God would be out of place. So why does he offer one? This is only one more instance of a deeper ambivalence in Descartes – one that we already ran into when we considered what he says of his idea of God. On the one hand, he often emphasizes the supremely exalted, or infinite, nature of the Divinity, insisting that it is beyond his grasp or comprehension. And if you reflect, that is the side in evidence in the espousal of the Grotean dictum, that God has "a supreme right" over human beings – the emphasis is on the enormous distance between God and us. We shall meet it again later, present again at an important moment, how to explain human freedom: once more Descartes will appeal to God's immensity, and to human inability to fully comprehend it.

But there is also the other side, the one that I earlier termed "prosaic" – I might well have called it "workmanlike" (see chapter 4). It surfaces often at no great distance from the idiom of immensity. God, insofar as Descartes has a clear idea and talks about him confidently, is really a master craftsman. In that capacity, we can rate the quality of his work – be satisfied, or inclined to complain. In that capacity too, axioms of fabrication apply to his products, not just the two that I have mentioned so far, but also this one:

No matter how skilled the craftsman, he does not have to put into each of his works all the perfections that he can put into some.

This, too, is in *Meditation Four* (AT 7, 56; CSM 2, 39) – only a few lines after the remark that "God's nature is immense, incomprehensible and infinite"! It is in the spirit of this third axiom that Descartes, after having described at length the features (or "perfections") that God could have put into him to counterbalance the gap between the two faculties involved in the passing of judgments, will appeal to considerations of cosmic richness and diversity to explain why God deliberately omitted to put those features into him, and so made it possible that he, Descartes, not always judge rightly but lapse into mistakes.

Something else goes with the vocabulary of craftsmanship, with the idiom of putting or not putting, of inserting or not inserting, of stamping or not stamping – remember, those words are the backbone of the argument about what God could have done. The words suggest an image. They encourage us to see ourselves as contraptions into which their maker has installed, or not installed, certain fixtures. This is not far distant from how I think about my bicycle – even though Descartes is only speaking about *mental* capacities. Much of *Meditation Four* is in tune with a vision of human beings as complicated mechanisms – bodiless of course, so far as Descartes can tell at this point. Call this a *mechanist* view of the mind.

But once again, this is only one face. There is the other, almost adjacent in the text. Descartes, and it is important to insist on this, never renounces the view that mistakes are privations: "in their formal definition, falsity and fault just consist in privation" (AT 7, 60–1; CSM 2, 42). So when I wrongly multiply 13 by 17 (my example) I am indeed deprived of what is owed to me – even though the privation "in no way requires the concurrence of God." Well, if God is uninvolved, who is it then that deprives me? Again Descartes is ultra-laconic, in fact confining himself to one remark a few lines before those that I have just quoted: "[T]he privation that constitutes the essence of error lies [*inest*] in the incorrect use of free will. It lies in the act itself, insofar as it proceeds from me [*in ipsa operatione, quatenus a me procedit*]" (AT 7, 60; CSM 2, 41). So: when I miscount 17 times 13, I do not just exhibit a limitation; I am deprived of what is owed to me. But who is the depriver? It isn't my prime maker, since the privation does not arise from my native constitution but "lies in the act itself insofar as it proceeds from me." We can only conclude that the depriver is – myself. Which brings us to two important points.

First, this announcement is a major corrective to the view suggested by the "putting into" – language of *Meditation Four*, the view that I am a sophisticated sort of machine. Look back to our last quote – to error residing in the act "insofar as it proceeds from me." When does an act proceed from me? Answer: when it was up to me whether to engage in it or not. It is a persistent view of Descartes' that there is error in the strict sense only where there is an "incorrect use of free will" – see again our quote above. This is what happens when I mis-multiply 13 by 17; but doesn't happen in other cases that Descartes keeps bringing to our attention, so as to contrast them with the standard kind. In the *Principles*, Part 4, article 196 (AT 8a, 320; CSM 1, 283),[10] he tells the story of a young woman who, unknown to herself, had had her arm amputated at the elbow and kept complaining of pain in her fingers, when in fact these no longer existed – I gather this is now called "phantom-limb experience." In *Meditation Six* (AT 7, 84; CSM 2, 58) the example is *dropsy*, a sickness where the patient craves drink even though drinking is bad for him. The young woman, the dropsical man, are not simply mistaken, Descartes will insist, they are being *deceived*. Deceived by whom, exactly? Not by God of course, since God is no deceiver; but by "a positive impulse derived from the nature that God has given [them] so as to preserve [their] body."[11] Let us not ask how the impulse preserves; nor even how God, in this situation, escapes the charge of deception. What matters is the insistence that these are not cases of plain error, not cases where the deluded have deprived themselves of the truth: someone or something has deprived them – "nature." They are victims, not agents. By contrast, when I miscount 17 times 13, I am an agent; the wrong answer is one that I have opted for; and opting isn't anything that a machine can do.

A second thought lurks in the talk of self-deprivation, also important. As we saw, when I deprive myself I fail to provide for myself what is my due, or what I owe to myself. Now "privation," "owing," "debt," "due" – these are all words well present in *Meditation Four*. By contrast, "debt to myself" is a phrase that Descartes' reader has to make up from that laconic proviso about privation inhering in the act "insofar as it proceeds from me." If we reflect, it is no surprise at all that the phrase should be absent: a century such as Descartes', where talk of rights rules the roost, will pay attention to what others owe to me, and to what I owe to others – and not to what I owe to myself. The mere fact that Descartes should voice the thought of self-debt, even if only indirectly, suggests that he does not fully share the prevalent Grotean vision, and does not primarily regard himself as a bearer of rights – one might even view him as an ancestor of Kant, and of the doctrine that humans beings have duties not just to others, but also to themselves.[12] When we come to his moral theory, we shall find more to support this conjecture; for the moment, let us simply retain the thought that for Descartes, there is an inherent wrong in every mistake we make – namely, we owed it to ourselves not to make it: a striking thought, surely. What is more, that fact, too, distances us from machines: perhaps (perhaps?) it is owed to my bicycle that its wheels not rub against the frame, but it is not something that the bicycle owes to itself. The debt is mine, or the mechanic's; bicycles don't owe themselves anything.

So, to look back, what has our *Meditation* detailed so far about error?

Well, I now know that God has not so rigged me as to be like a clock that always tells the wrong time: my faculties "tend toward the truth." Still, has he not so created me that I often make mistakes – I may believe that the earth is flat, or that 464,731 is a prime number, or like Snow White, that this apple is good to eat?[13] The answer is: yes and no. Yes, he could have so made me that I had none of these beliefs – in that sense, God may be said to "have a share" (*concurrere*) in my errors (AT 7, 60; CSM 2, 41). But in a deeper sense, God is not responsible – most of the errors I make are really *mine*: I misuse the faculties that God has given me, and the misuse originates in me alone.

Still, to understand this assignment of responsibilities we need to see how beliefs arise in the first place, and how they go astray. This is what Descartes discusses in the central pages of *Meditation Four*; I now turn to them.

idealization

Y ou ask me the time. I look at my watch and say "three-thirty," truthfully, thinking it so. Or you ask, is 131 a prime number? I work it out in my head and reply "yes," again truthfully, again thinking it so. According to Descartes, this thinking – not just my looking, or my working it out, or my saying the words – no, the sheer thought that things are actually thus has in both instances involved an act of my will. How so? What I have called *thinking* Descartes calls *judging*, in line with philosophic usage of his time; in today's professional jargon one would more likely speak of my *believing*, or *holding*, that it was three-thirty, or that 131 was a prime number. Be that as it may, in Cartesian parlance I have judged these things; and a doctrine first voiced in *Meditation Four* and never renounced afterward, has it that whenever we judge, two mental acts occur – an act of intellect and an act of the will. Once again, the plainest statement is in the Jesuit-destined textbook, the *Principles of Philosophy*, at article 34 of Part 1, whose title is: *That the will, as well as the intellect, is needed for judging.* It begins like this:

> The intellect [*intellectus*] is needed for judging, since we cannot judge what we in no way grasp [*nullo modo percipimus*]; but the will [*voluntas*] is also needed, so that assent be given [*assensio præbeatur*] to what is in some way [*aliquo modo*] grasped. (AT 8a, 18; CSM 1, 204)

Two components, then, must be present for a judgment to occur. Let us try and figure out how they work.

From the moment it was first put forward, this doctrine has had an aura of paradox; in fact it has seemed downright perverse, obviously false even. The third *Objector*, Hobbes, put it like this (*Third* set, *Objection* 13: AT 7, 192; CSM 2, 134):

> [T]o know that something is true – or even believe it, or give it one's assent – has nothing to do with the will [*aliena sunt a voluntate*]; for we believe willy-nilly [*volentes nolentes credimus*] what is proved to us by valid argument, or told on credible grounds. True enough, asserting or denying,

maintaining or refuting a proposition, are acts of the will [*actus volun-tatis*]; but it does not follow on that account that inner assent [*assensu[s] internu[s]*] depends on the will [*depende[t] a voluntate*].

As you may have sensed, some words and phrases of this rebuttal are less innocent than they appear: *acts of* the will, or *depends on* the will. Or – *the will*, for that matter. Take this last: it is not a word we should take for granted. The ancient Greeks, for example, did without it – one would be hard put to translate our article 1–34 into Aristotle's Greek. And almost as hard put, I'm tempted to say, into present-day plain English. Yes, there is the adverb: you had to agree *willy-nilly* that 131 was a prime. And the participle: I might have been *willing* or *unwilling* to answer your questions. And the noun: I might have shown *good will* as I answered them; you may have divulged my answers to someone else *against my will*. We might speak of there being no *political will* in this country to give adequate support to people with disabilities. But has the verb a straight indicative form in plain English, except when it means "bequeath"? Does the noun occur as a subject, alone and countable, except when it means "testament"? *My* will? *The* will? In the *Twilight of the Idols* Nietzsche derides philosophers for sighting an "inner world" which they then populate with phantoms and will-o'-the-wisps – "the will" being a prime denizen.[1] It would be strange, wouldn't it, if you asked me to look inward and ascertain whether I had, or had not, used my will as I judged that 131 was a prime number. How would I go about looking? What mental micro-chip would I be searching for? Suppose we grant at least a milder version of Nietzsche's charge: that the will – though not quite a phantom – is a philosophical kaleidoscope, many shapes to be glimpsed. Which one is in your sight when you insist, Descartes-like, that I exerted my will even as I judged that 131 was a prime? Or inversely, what stance of mind are you intent on contrasting this judgment with? By looking for affinities and contrasts, we might hope to discern what was at stake in the debate between Descartes and his English *Objector*.

Still, why are we at first inclined to side with Hobbes's thrust, almost intuitively it seems? The likely answer is this: to the extent that we accept to speak of the will at all, we tend (like Hobbes) to regard it as a faculty of *choice*. The will comes into play when "it's up to me" what I do; and (like Hobbes) we are inclined to suppose that once I have worked it out, it is not up to me what I think of 131. *Volentes nolentes credimus*: we believe willy-nilly. There is no choice in the matter.

Did Descartes say that there was? Well, yes – some of the time; as, for instance, in a 1645 *letter* to Mesland, whose exact import has been a matter of debate among Cartesian scholars. Here it is:

> [W]hen a very evident reason moves us one way, even though morally speaking we can hardly move in the other direction, absolutely speaking we can. For it is always up to us [*semper nobis licet*] to hold back from . . . admitting a clear truth, provided we think it good to prove the freedom of our will by doing so. (Feb. 9: AT 4, 173; CSMK, 245)

"It is always up to us to hold back": this seems clear enough. Alas, the waters are more troubled elsewhere, especially in *Meditation Four*, where the doctrine that judging equals willing is advanced for the first time. For there, Descartes says three things. One (AT 7, 58; CSM 2, 40), that I judge 131 to be prime (my example) once I made the calculation, because God "so sets up" (*ita disponit*) the "inner workings of my thought" (*intima cogitationis meæ*) – the language of fabrication, we know it well. He also says (AT 7, 60; CSM 2, 42) that this judgment is an act of will (*actus voluntatis*); and thirdly (AT 7, 56; CSM 2, 39), that will is a faculty of choice (*facultas eligendi*). So we have the standard characterization; but it is hard to escape the feeling that it comes here as a sort of honorary label; or even perhaps in the train of some other vision of how "will" infuses our beliefs.

The feeling becomes even more inescapable as we take in another tenet of Cartesianism, which emerges mainly in the *Correspondence*. Descartes was very sensitive to a charge sometimes leveled at him, that when he had as much as supposed that God might be a deceiver, he had committed an act of impiety. His line of defense is unwavering: there is a world of difference, he says, between *supposing* something and *asserting* it. And what difference, exactly? "Supposition . . . is an act of the intellect and not of the will" (*letter* to the curators of the University of Leiden, May 4, 1647 (AT 5, 9; CSMK, 316); and likewise four years earlier, in a *letter* to Buitendijk (AT 4, 64; CSMK, 229)). So be it. And yet – and yet: is it not in my power to suppose anything I please? What could be more a matter of choice – more "up to me" – than *that*? Nonetheless and quite categorically Descartes declares supposition to be no act of will. How not to conclude, therefore, that he did not regard will as predominantly a faculty of choice, even though he also viewed it as that, sometimes anyway?

What else, then, was the will for Descartes? Go back to our text of the *Principles*: "will is needed, in order that we give assent." So here is the name for the mental act that requires a will for its performance, and that occurs whenever we pass judgment: we assent. Judging, or *believing* as we now call it, involves assenting. After 1640 Descartes never swerved from this doctrine: only mentioned in passing in *Meditation Four* (AT 7, 59; CSM 2, 41 – again at AT 7, 61; CSM 2, 41), it becomes almost a dogma from then on. For example, in a pamphlet of 1648, the so-called

Comments on a Certain Broadsheet written to disown a former disciple, Regius, one of the heresies chalked up against Regius is that he holds judgments to be acts of intellect, whereas he (Descartes) "assigned the act of judging itself, which consists simply in assenting . . . to the determination of the will" (AT 8b, 363; CSM 1, 307). Perhaps Descartes felt some residual pressure to hold that for assent to be an act *of* will, it had also to be bestow-able *at* will; this would explain the 1645 letter to Mesland, which I quoted a page ago. But in many texts, not just in *Meditation Four* but elsewhere, in the *Comments* for example, the two are set apart; and Hobbes's attack misses the mark by overlooking the separation. Something do-able at will – e.g. supposing that God is a deceiver – need not on that account be an act of the will; and conversely an act of the will – e.g. assenting to the proposition that 131 is prime – need not be something do-able at will. Let's take *this*, and not the letter of 1645, as mainstream Cartesian doctrine. Still, what is assent?

To my knowledge, Descartes never answers this question, at least not when he discusses belief or judgment. Perhaps he took the notion to be self-evident; or he seemed to, almost to the end of his life. Fortunately we have one text, late, where assent reappears and is not treated as a matter of course; a text far removed from *Meditation Four* and from the *Principles* – far removed (it would seem) from any of their concerns. Here it is:

> Love is an emotion of the soul . . . that incites it to join itself by will [*se joindre de volonté*] to objects that seem suitable [*convenables*] to it. . . . By the word "will," I mean here not desire – which is a different passion, directed to the future – but the assent [*consentement*] by which you consider yourself from this very moment so joined to what you love that you imagine a whole of which you think yourself but one part, and the object of your love the other.

The topic is *love*; and the lines just quoted belong to that last and less read work of Descartes, which he devoted to feelings and emotions and called the *Passions of the Soul* – these are sections 79 and 80, where love is first defined and explained (AT 11, 387; CSM 1, 356). Merging and simplifying and taking *consentement* to be French for *assensio*, one might say that Descartes' view comes to this: to love is to assent.

More important for our purposes, we are also told something about assent. *Consentir* means: to consider yourself so joined to someone that you and that person form one unit. As a theorist of love, Descartes stands of course in a lineage; for quite apart from its literal aptness, the image of *making-oneself-one-with-someone-else* has a long literary history. Think only of Aristophanes' tale in Plato's *Symposium*: those spheric creatures, our ancestors, cleft in two by the jealous gods, each half forever fated to search for the other, the halves sometimes fortunate enough to succeed in their quest – love, the rapturous embrace of their long-sought reunion.[2] A haunting myth. Still, Descartes does a lot more than simply reword the tale; he softens its darker hues. He allows us, for example, to speak of *love past*. Human beings do not just fall in love, they fall out of it too – or so we say. But how to say it, if you are Aristophanes? Take Jason, the leader of the Argonauts, who is now abandoning his wife Medea. What to say of these two? Only this, it seems: that *he*, now deserting her, cannot have loved *her* – ever. He had not found in her his other half, he only thought he had; it was not love, only (for a while) its mirage. Incidentally, the same holds for *her*, for the same reasons. Descartes of course can speak differently; his vision does not call for this gloomy appraisal, since it transposes the Aristophanic formula onto the *intentional* mode (I speak philosophic jargon now). Before his fall into indifference, Jason may well have joined himself "by will" to Medea. He may have considered himself part of a whole, whose other part she was. It may have been love, genuine love. Sadly, he so considers himself no longer. We might say that, perhaps, for Descartes the verb "love" conjugates also in the past – albeit sparingly. Can Don Giovanni have "thought himself one" with the 1,003 Spanish ladies of Leporello's list? The specter of Aristophanes' spherical creatures forbids us to believe *that*.

Let me now import a word, post-*dixseptiémiste* though it may be. Let me say that for Descartes, to love is *to be committed* – that is what "assent" comes to in the end. I realize the import rings trendy and Sartrean and modern, yet it is not an inapt rendering of what is involved in considering oneself so joined to someone that you and that person form one unit. Don't articles 79 and 80 of the *Passions*, doesn't the word "commitment," describe well enough Jason's early stance toward Medea? Grant that they do, and return to the matter of will. Since Descartes regards assent as *the* characteristic activity of will, it seems proper to say that he regards will as first and foremost a faculty of commitment; and so, that he regards it as a faculty of attitudes, or at any rate some attitudes. (Do not rush to say "attitudes, period": after all, detachment is an attitude too.)

Now for another neologism, as far as Descartes is concerned. Begin with some lines written near his time, in fact less than a score years after the *Passions*:

> The pale-faced lady's lily-white, perforce;
> The swarthy one's a sweet brunette, of course;
> The spindly lady has a slender grace;
> The fat one has a most majestic pace;
> The plain one, with her dress in disarray,

> They classify as *beauté négligée*;
> The hulking one's a goddess in their eyes,
> The dwarf a concentrate of Paradise;
> The haughty lady has a noble mind;
> The mean one's witty, and the dull one's kind;
> The chatterbox has liveliness and verve,
> The mute one has a virtuous reserve.
> So lovers manage, in their passion's cause,
> To love their ladies even for their flaws.

This is comic verse, of course, not philosophy: a young woman, Eliante, is berating Alceste – the *misanthrope* – for his insistence on absolute honesty. Nor are the words new: Molière is knowingly paraphrasing Lucretius.[3] One might add too, that Eliante's catalogue chronicles a homespun truth, that love is no friend of lucidity. Let me give this fact a name coined by a thinker more of our time – this is the neologism I announced:

> [I]n connection with this question of being in love we have always been struck by the phenomenon of sexual over-evaluation – the fact that the loved object enjoys a certain amount of freedom from criticism, and that all its characteristics are valued more highly than those of people who are not loved, or than its own were at a time when it itself was not loved. . . . The tendency which falsifies judgment in this respect is that of *idealization*.

The writer is Freud;[4] and to illustrate this "tendency," here is a fragment of autobiography:

> As a child I was in love with a girl of my own age, who was slightly cross-eyed. The imprint made on my brain by these wayward eyes became so mingled with whatever else had aroused in me the feeling of love that for years afterwards, when I saw a cross-eyed woman, I was more prone to love her than any other, simply for that flaw – all the while not knowing this was the reason. But then I reflected and realized it *was* a flaw: I am smitten no longer.

So be it – except that these confidences come not from Freud or one of his clients, they belong to Descartes, imparted to Queen Christina *via* the French attaché in Stockholm (*letter* to Chanut, June 6, 1647: AT 5, 57; CSMK, 322). The Queen had asked, why do we love one person rather than another before knowing their merit? It can be because of an imprint on the brain, Descartes replies; and tells his tale. But *cause* is only one part of the story. "No matter how unbalanced [*déréglé*], love has always the good for its object," says an earlier letter, again to the Queen via Chanut (February 1, 1647: AT 4, 614; CSMK, 312). And here, "object" is of course to be understood *intentionally* (again, apologies for jargon). It means: what we love, we *take* to be good. Descartes does not divulge quite how he felt about cross-eyes before his self-analysis – were they a charm in their own right? Or did those faces radiate wit, verve, fantasy? No matter, that love was *déréglé*. And, as it happens, "*déréglé*" is the word standardly affixed, from the seventeenth century onward, to a machine (say, a clock) that no longer works properly and needs readjustment: manifestly, a word with a future.

Let me for my part bestow a longer past to that other word – Freud's – and say that for Descartes, too, love crucially involves idealization. Take again the February 1647 letter to Christina, via Chanut: "[love] makes the soul imagine lovable qualities in objects in which, at another time, it would see nothing but faults" (AT 4, 603; CSMK, 307). Of course many have, across the centuries, voiced similar thoughts – plain folk, poets, moralists. Yet even so, Descartes stands out, for he turns this singular fact about one feeling into a basic fact of our mental make-up.

How so? Begin by supposing that the tendency to idealize is a trait which goes *naturally* with that other stance constitutive of loving – making-oneself-one with the beloved. The two go together in the sense that they are twin aspects of the same power or faculty, at work when we love a person. As it happens (so Descartes thinks), we have given that faculty a name, we call it "the will" – remember article 79 of the *Passions*: "love is an emotion of the soul . . . that incites it to join itself by will [*de volonté*] to objects that seem suitable to it."[5] It was *will*, then, that made Descartes "assent" to the girl with the wayward eyes; *will*, too, that made him see those eyes as enchanting or mysterious. If you reflect, there is no logical necessity for these two attitudes to go together – could we not imagine creatures that found no special charm or merit in the one they loved? They would simply be unlike us human beings, who are so constituted that our will is at once a faculty of commitment and of idealization.

Proceed a little further now, keeping this last assignment in your sights. Descartes sees eyes that focus disparately, he falls in love with a vivacious face. He has idealized – gone beyond – what he actually grasped. If we accept (and why not?) this idiom of "going beyond," and also allocate acts to faculties, it will be natural enough to say that in this instance one faculty has gone beyond the other; and giving them their due names, say that the *will* has gone beyond the *intellect*. In fact we may say even more. It was wayward eyes that beguiled Descartes; for someone else, it might be a croaky voice, or sticking-out ears, or whatever. No feature, it seems, is beyond idealization, no one beyond being loved by someone. I may be utterly ill-served by fortune, utterly bereft of merit or attraction, a braying donkey in fact – and adored by a Queen:

recall *A Midsummer Night's Dream*? Against this horizon of possibilities, does it not seem natural to say that human power to idealize is limitless? infinite? and so say not only that will *outstrips* intellect, but that it is, even in us, *infinite*?

Observe how little this train of thought has turned on viewing will as a faculty of choice. Yes, Descartes "went beyond" what he saw; but this hardly means that his extra step was to make a choice – that he chose to view crossed eyes as a charm; or chose to be in love, falsely so viewing them. It is a spell that makes Titania swoon over an ass's brayings.[6] *Un amour déréglé*, if ever there was one. Which are we to suppose, however: that the spell made her mis-hear, hence swoon – or swoon, hence mis-hear? The second, surely; and remember, spells (as stories have them) are often merely our own selves – cast outward. "We neither strive for, nor will, nor want, nor desire anything because we judge it to be good; on the contrary, we judge a thing to be good because we strive for, or will, or want, or desire it." True, these are not Descartes' words but Spinoza's;[7] but Spinoza is often the philosopher who speaks in Descartes' voice, or at least one of his voices.

This said, have I not made too much of one sentence and two letters? Remember, in the entire opus (so far as I know) it is only in section 80 of the *Passions* that Descartes uses the idiom of *joining-oneself-with* to describe what assent is;[8] and only in the letters of February and June 1647 to the Queen via Chanut that he stresses the idealizing bent of lovers. One published sentence here, two bits of correspondence there – are these not feeble grounds on which to credit Descartes with a theory of the will that makes it first and foremost a power of *commitment-cum-idealization*? Narrow, I shall grant; but not feeble on that account. Throughout the 1647 letters, love is defined as in the *Passions*, as the "joining oneself by will" with another person. If two years later, Descartes affixed to that joining the word he had pervasively used to stand for the act of will that generates beliefs, namely "assent," it can hardly be *à la légère*; he must have come to think that love and belief resembled one another – they were both "joinings," generically; and the same psychic mechanism was at work in them both. What's more, there can be little doubt that Descartes was further swayed in his resolve to assimilate the two by the fact that "idealization" (as I am calling it here, thanks to Freud) had been a mainstay of his account of will, from the start.

Go back to *Meditation Four* where the doctrine which, since Hobbes's day, has struck many readers as perverse, is voiced for the first time. We are told (AT 7, 60; CSM 2, 42) that beliefs ("judgments") are acts of will (*actus voluntatis*); also (AT 7, 56; CSM 2, 39), that the will is bound by no limits (*nullis limitibus circumscribi[tur]*); and also (AT 7, 58; CSM 2,

40), that it ranges wider than the intellect (*latius pate[t] quam intellectus*). Hobbes, as we saw, demurred at the "acts of will"; another *Objector*, Gassendi, was more puzzled by the "ranging-wider": "the will never applies to anything which the intellect has not already perceived," he objected (*Fifth* set of *Objections*: AT 7, 314; CSM 2, 218). Here is how Descartes replied (AT 7, 376–7; CSM 2, 259):

> You want me to say in a few words what the will can apply to, that is beyond the intellect? Briefly: to everything in which we happen to go wrong. . . . When you judge that an apple (which happens to be poisoned) will suit you as food, you grasp well enough that its smell, color and the like are pleasant; this does not mean you grasp that the apple is healthy as food. But because you so will, you so judge. . . . We can will a forest where there is only a tree.[9]

Not *amour déréglé* but *jugement déréglé* this time; yet the dynamics are much the same. Then Descartes saw wayward eyes – and fell in love with an intriguing face; now Gassendi smells a sweet fragrance, sees shiny red skin – and believes a certain apple will be good to eat. Love has taken the lover – and belief, the believer – beyond what they actually grasped. In both cases there is an extra step; call "will" the power that enabled them to take it. *Quia ita vis, ita judicas.* Because you so will, you so judge – it is important to understand this dictum aright. Descartes is NOT saying (as CSM make him say): "because you want to believe it, you judge [that the apple will be beneficial]." But rather: "because you want in a certain way, you judge [that the apple will be beneficial]." And here, "want in a certain way" (*ita vis*) means: commit yourself ("assent," "join yourself by will") to a certain state of affairs, or to a certain course of action. "State of affairs," "course of action"; these are of course modern phrases – Descartes would simply speak of "object." It being three-thirty is a state of affairs; eating an apple, a course of action. Note also that Descartes' example to Gassendi cunningly straddles the line between knowledge and behavior: it is not simply a matter of what Gassendi believes about the apple, but whether he decides to bite too.

As we assent, so we love or believe or decide; and as we love or believe or decide, so we see. In a person we love, we shall see merit; in a course of action we decide on, good; in a state of affairs in which we believe, truth. A few lines after the poisoned apple, Descartes offers a formula which one might almost take to define what assent is. *Cum prave judicamus, non ideo prave volumus, sed forte pravum quid:* "when we judge wrong, it is not that we will wrong; but we will what happens to be wrong." If you reflect, that is the exact pendant of the February 1647 remark to Chanut which I quoted above (p. 91) – that love, however *déréglé*, always had the good for its object. We might say that Titania loved wrongly, meaning: she joined-herself-by-will to someone who happened to be ill-suited. And just as it is with our loves, there is hardly a limit to how *déréglés* our beliefs and decisions can be. We can all be Titanias, willing a forest where there is only a tree.

However, that is not the end of the story – Descartes' doctrine is more complicated; he discerns yet a further dimension in the will, crucial for the acquiring of beliefs. To explain, I shall once more focus on examples, in particular on two that I have already canvassed: my answering "yes" to your question whether 131 was a prime number; and Gassendi's mis-judgment about the apple.

We have here two instances of believing which are quite different. It isn't that one belief is accurate while the other is not: *that* imparity in no way affects the role that the will plays in their genesis. Gassendi might have happened to be right in his opinion of the apple's nutritiousness – the apple might not have been poisoned. Yet his will would still have played the same role in his coming to believe as he did; it would still have "extended further" than his intellect; in my usage, Gassendi would still have idealized what he saw. As for the other aspect so far distin-guished in the mental act of willing, namely assent – making-oneself-one with what one believes – it is obviously present both in my answer about 131, and in Gassendi's eagerness to taste the apple.

No, the difference on which Descartes fastens lies elsewhere; it has to do with how *clearly* the believer, in our two examples, grasps what he believes. About 131: once I have gone through the requisite steps (i.e. ascertained that 131 is almost equal to 12^2 but not divisible without remainder by any prime between 1 and 12), I have as clear an idea as anyone could wish to have of its status as a prime number. Things are in a different league, however, with Gassendi's apple. As Descartes points out, Gassendi may see clearly enough that the apple looks good and smells good, but this does not amount to his having a clear vision that it is healthy – in fact, one might have a hard time specifying what would constitute a clear vision of *that*. Using Cartesian idiom, we might say that there is this difference, then, between the two situations: I (answer-ing about 131) have a clear and distinct idea of what I believe; Gassendi (observing the apple) does not.

Why does it matter? Think back to the question asked in the last chap-ter, bearing in mind that it is within its context that belief is discussed throughout our *Meditation*. The question was this: had Descartes the right to complain that God had so made him as to be prone to countless mistakes? You may remember, the answer was *no* – because typically when Descartes made a mistake, the act "proceeded from him," and involved an "incorrect use of free will" (AT 7, 60; CSM 2, 41). Switch back now, and ask: how do these descriptions fit Gassendi's judgment of the apple? Exactly in what sense does the mistake proceed from him? How does free-will enter the picture? Descartes' answer is simple: since Gassendi lacks a clear and distinct idea of what he is judging about, he has in effect *opted* to believe as he does. This does not necessarily mean that he engaged in deliberation before believing; rather, before he came to believe as he did, he was in a state of *indifference*. That noun (or the corresponding adjective) occurs about half a dozen times in the middle pages of our *Meditation* (AT 7, 58–9; CSM 2, 40–1), and has almost a technical meaning: it harks back to scholastic idiom, where it was sometimes even amplified into "indifference of equipoise." I am indifferent with respect to a course of action when there is no reason why I should engage in it rather than not. For example, should I believe rather than disbelieve that on September 13, 2440 it will rain where I now stand? I know nothing that is relevant to an answer, so am equally inclined toward *yes* and *no* – I am indifferent. Now you might object, surely that is not Gassendi's situation *vis-à-vis* the apple. He is not in a state of total ignorance: the apple looks fresh, smells gorgeous, is proffered by a kind-looking donor. However:

> [I]ndifference does not merely apply to cases where the intellect is wholly ignorant, but extends in general to every case where the intellect does not have sufficiently clear knowledge at the time when the will deliberates. For although probable conjectures may pull me in one direction, the mere knowledge that they are simply conjectures, and not certain and indubitable reasons, is itself quite enough to push my assent the other way. (AT 7, 59; CSM 2, 41)

Gassendi's perception of the apple's integrity is not clear; so, on the view just enunciated, he *is* indifferent about what to believe. Let us not quarrel with this contention; but a troubling consequence seems to follow.

Suppose you have no reason whatever to act one way rather than the other; yet you do end up acting one way. Your course, then, was not caused by any factor that anyone, however well informed, could have singled out before your action. We might say: it was a *chance* event. Or alternatively we might say that, no, it wasn't chance: the course originated in you, or to use a verb that we have met recently, it *proceeded from* you; and in the same vein, we might say that the deciding factor was your *free-will*, or *liberum arbitrium* (if we speak Latin). In that vein, we might also speak of free-will as a faculty – a power that enables an act to emanate from an agent, uncaused, unnecessitated by previous events or conditions. Descartes clearly speaks of it thus.

Again, let us not quarrel, and accept to view free-will as this power of absolute origination, sometimes at work in human beings. We shall say, then, that Gassendi's free-will was a decisive factor in his coming to believe that the apple would be nutritious. But now we face a problem.

Return to my answer about 131. As I think of that number once I have done my calculations, there is no question of my being indifferent; no question, it seems, of my needing an act of free-will to originate my belief. Why not? Because (as we have seen – AT 7, 58; CSM 2, 40) God has "so set up the inner workings of my thought" that I instantly believe any proposition that I grasp clearly and distinctly: to borrow Hobbes's phrase, I do it *willy-nilly*. So we seem to be confronted with the awkward (or exciting?) conclusion that our mistakes exhibit our freedom, while our truest beliefs are mere displays of an inner mechanism (by "truest," I mean those beliefs that don't just *happen* to be true: after all, Gassendi might have been right about the apple). And the same, presumably, holds of vice and virtue: I am free when I sin, but a mere slave of my nature when I do right.

As we might expect, this conclusion would not exactly appeal to Descartes. He avoids it by making a further distinction:

> The will or freedom of decision . . . simply consists in our ability to do or not to do (i.e. affirm or deny, pursue or avoid); or rather it consists simply in the fact that when the intellect puts something forward for affirmation or denial or for pursuit or avoidance, our inclination is such that we do not feel we are determined by any external force. (AT 7, 57; CSM 2, 40)

Let me, in this text, alter a phrase that has caused problems for Descartes' readers – the "or rather" (*vel potius*) that stands between the two clauses about what free-will simply consists in. Let us slightly change the disjunction and write instead "or else" – to make clear that we take Descartes to be offering not two accounts of one thing, but one account of two things. On this reading, then, there are two kinds of situation where I can be said to have acted freely: (a) I was indifferent beforehand – I could "do or not do"; or (b) I was uncompelled – I did not "feel I was determined by any outside force." There is free-will and free-will, then. It is in sense (a) that Gassendi believes freely. But my belief about 131 is free too, not because I am indifferent (as we have seen, I am not); but because I want to think as I do, and feel no external compulsion to do so – this is sense (b). Descartes uses again a term of art to designate this second sort of freedom, he calls it "spontaneity" (AT 7, 59; CSM 2, 41): so far from judging willy-nilly, I hold spontaneously that 131 is prime.

To sum up, then. Having a belief engages the will not merely as a faculty of assent, it also involves free-will: most of our beliefs are arrived at *freely*. This seems a reasonable tenet, if we want to distinguish normal forming of an opinion from say, being brainwashed, or deceived by one's nature – feeling pain, for example, in a finger that one has lost. Perhaps reasonable too, is a ranking that Descartes introduces in connection with these freedoms:

the indifference I feel when there is no reason pushing me one way rather than the other, is the lowest grade of freedom; it is evidence not of any perfection in that freedom, but only of a defect in knowledge or a kind of negation. (AT 7, 58; CSM 2, 40)

As we know, Descartes likes to rank; and given that acting from indifference is not all that far removed from acting randomly, it seems plausible to view indifference as a low grade of freedom, perhaps even as a "kind of negation."

So, to look back on *Meditation Four* as a whole: it appears as though Descartes has, after all, absolved God of responsibility for our mistakes. They issue from just ourselves, from that low-grade freedom which we possess, *indifference* – low-grade not because it is limited in scope, but because it is akin to randomness. But we also enjoy a higher grade, which we display whenever we act or think rightly: in those situations we are *spontaneously* free, we do as we want, nothing is imposed on us from outside.

Yet once again, there is more to be said. Attractive and plausible though it may look, our *Meditation* has often left academic readers of Descartes uneasy, not because of what is there, but because of what is – or is not – elsewhere in the *corpus*. Clearly, Descartes never changed his mind about assent: we find an exact parallel of the *Meditation* in the *Principles* (look at the quote at the beginning of this chapter); and as we saw, will-as-a-faculty-of-assent is taken to be a crucial component of love in Descartes' final work, the *Passions of the Soul*. It is a different matter, though, when we turn to free-will – a kind of gap seems to have opened between what we are told in our *Meditation*, and what appears in the later work.[10] I shall return to this subject in the final chapter of this book, where I discuss feelings and morality; for it will turn out that in the *Passions* (article 153: AT 11, 445–6; CSM 1, 384), Descartes singles out consciousness of free-will as the basis of a feeling that governs proper moral relations between human beings – he calls it "generosity." More to come, then; here, however, are some interim remarks.

First, it is clear that the topic of free-will continued to preoccupy Descartes: as we have just seen, it will reappear at an important moment of the *Passions*; and in the *Principles*, seven articles are devoted to it – Part 1, articles 37–43 (AT 8a, 18–21; CSM 1, 205–7). What is more, this is a topic copiously discussed in Descartes' century; so he can hardly have helped knowing that his words would be scanned by practiced eyes; and variations, no matter how small, would not escape notice. Given these circumstances, we should take note of at least some curious deviations. The first concerns the "higher" grade of freedom which Descartes, in our *Meditation*, contrasts so starkly with indifference: spontaneity, or absence of external compulsion. Remember, the existence of that freedom is crucial to the thesis that when we believe in a clearly perceived truth, we believe freely. Well, in the later work, spontaneity receives hardly any mention, perhaps even none. The *Principles* speak of freedom, period; and discuss questions such as these: whether freedom of the will is self-evident (1–39), or how that freedom can be reconciled with divine preordination (1–41) – questions which all presuppose that by "freedom," one means the ability to do or not to do, i.e. indifference. Why is spontaneity ignored? An even more pressing question arises when we set our *Meditation* text beside the *Passions* passage that introduces generosity. As I have mentioned, according to Descartes that feeling arises from the realization that we have "mastery" (*empire*) over our volitions: obviously, power to-do-or-not-to-do is what is being talked about – again, indifference. And we read (article 152) that this mastery "makes us in some way similar to God" (*nous rend en quelque façon semblables à Dieu*). Really? How does this diagnosis square with the low grade bestowed on indifference in *Meditation Four*? Is there perhaps indifference and indifference – some higher, some lower? or has Descartes perhaps even abandoned the idea of ranking free-wills? Whatever the answer, it does look as though the thoughts on freedom expressed in *Meditation Four* are but a stage toward a more complicated Cartesian vision.

I shall end this perusal of *Meditation Four* with a look at a verdict that Descartes does not pronounce till the *Meditation* that follows, though it is in fact a corollary of the proof with which *Meditation Four* began, that God is no deceiver. It deserves attention, I think, because it is more than a side note: it weaves together concerns and attitudes that we have met again and again as we followed Descartes on his course; concerns, obviously, that run deep in his psyche – relating to trust, fabrication, and rank.

Rank? Hardly a *Meditation* has passed without it coming up, in one form or another. In *Meditation One* we were told that atheists must view themselves as less perfect, hence less secure in their knowledge, than believers do – even believers who fear that they may be always deceived (AT 7, 21; CSM 2, 14). In *Meditation Two*, when Descartes experienced what he saw or smelled as qualities *of* the wax, while animals did not, again the difference led to a ranking: Descartes was more perfect than animals (AT 7, 32; CSM 2, 22). And of course, ideas can be ranked for their sophistication or "objective reality" – this is what enabled Descartes to offer the proof of God of *Meditation Three*. In *Meditation Four* we are made to wonder how a high-level craftsman such as God could have made a low-level product such as Descartes, beset by countless mistakes – a paradox which prompts the study that absorbs the *Meditation*, about the nature of human beliefs and how they go wrong.

Rank often comes interwoven with that other thread, fabrication – as in the *Meditation Four* paradox that I have just mentioned, about God's having made a faulty product. The two notions are also entwined in the low self-image assigned to the atheist in *Meditation One*: the image is low, because the atheist must view himself as the product of blind forces. They are again entwined in the proof of God of *Meditation Three* – it all turns on Descartes finding an idea that he could not have made up himself. Fabricators are indeed centre-stage in the *Meditations*. God is one: our world is his product, and it includes Descartes – with this and that feature installed into him. Descartes too is a fabricator: he crafts at least some of his ideas. And of course, fabricators are also on stage in the guise that they will soon don in common speech[11] – as purveyors of deceit. It is difficult not to link the omnipresence of deceit in the *Meditations* with the fact that, in the *Meditations'* century, fabrication has come to be closely identified in people's minds with the making of machines – machines being of course prime instruments of potential trickery. They can be engineered to provide false information – a clock, for instance, rigged to tell the wrong time; and more threateningly still, they can be crafted to look like non-machines – automata outside my window, made to behave like human beings, wearing hats and coats! Machinery opens new vistas for trust and distrust.

As for these two, they have been a presence from the start. Remember the first page of the *Meditations*, with its precept not to trust fully those who have deceived you even once. This gave birth to Cartesian doubt, that generic distrust of one's certainties. And now that the doubt has been conquered, finally and officially, with the proof that God does not deceive, trust returns to the fore, embedded in the mental act that is at the centre of knowledge and certainty. Belief, as *Meditation Four* has insisted, turns on *assent*, the act of making-oneself-one with what one has grasped. Assent isn't just given to propositions or courses of action; it can be given to people, when we love them (see again article 80 of the *Passions*) or when we trust them: these are kindred ways of making-one-self-one with another person. Nor is the kinship lost on Descartes: in an article of the *Passions* close to the ones that describe love (169: AT 11, 458; CSM 1, 390), Descartes, writing about blamable jealousy, remarks that the jealous husband, had he felt true love (*un vrai amour*) for his wife, would have had no inclination to distrust her (*aucune inclination à s'en défier*). So: love and trust go together, they are assents. But we should ask about another matter in the article that I have just mentioned, namely the standard by which the faulty husband is assessed: he lacks *true* love, we are told. What is that, exactly?

Think back to Aristophanes' tale of the spheric creatures cleft in two by the worried gods: the image of making-oneself-one with one's beloved goes back at least to that myth. Taken seriously, the myth rules out talk of *un amour passé* – *passé* in the sense of being felt yesterday, but no longer today: love gone, Aristophanists must hold, is love that never was, only its semblance. Jason and Medea have not loved truly; only Héloïse and Abélard have. Call this view *immutabilist* – love, once it has blossomed, does not fade.

Descartes, of course, is not committed to Aristophanic immutabilism – he nowhere writes that love is the fusion of split halves. Whether he nonetheless views lovers in that fashion is difficult to tell: he does not say enough. But if not from lovers, he certainly demands immutability from a breed that shares with them the dependence on trust and assent: *knowers*. Knowing involves being certain, which involves believing, which involves assenting. Let me take again the example of Euclid's theorem about primes – it is close enough to the kind that Descartes discusses. The Cartesian view is that no matter how convinced I am today of the infinite number of prime numbers, if I should doubt that infinity *tomorrow*, I do not know it *today*:

> [E]ven at the moment when you deduced [it] from clear principles, you did not have *knowledge* of it, but only a *conviction*. I distinguish the two as follows: there is conviction [*persuasio*] when there remains some reason which might lead you to doubt, but knowledge [*scientia*] is a conviction based on a reason so strong that it can never be shaken by any stronger reason.

This is in a *letter* of May 24, 1640 to Regius (AT 3, 65; CSMK, 147); and is reasserted at the end of *Meditation Five*:

> [O]ften the memory of a previously made judgment comes back to me when I am no longer attending to the arguments that led me to make it. And so other arguments can occur which might easily undermine my opinion if I did not have knowledge of God; and I should thus never have true and certain knowledge [*veram et certam scientiam*] of anything, but only shifting and mutable opinions. (AT 7, 69; CSM 2, 48)

A quick reminder: why does knowledge of God prevent the erosion of past certainties? Because it carries the assurance that our intellect "must tend toward the truth." Yesterday, before going through the travails of *Meditation Three* and *Four*, I lacked that assurance. So yesterday, if I remembered Euclid's theorem without recalling its proof, I might have been visited by doubts about my mental powers; and as a result, visited by doubts about the theorem itself. And had I not gone through the travails of the *Meditations*, I might be so visited tomorrow – or in 10 years. If these relapses can happen, then, according to the view enunciated by *Meditation Five*, I lacked knowledge of the theorem *even as I proved it*, 30 years ago.

But aren't there atheist mathematicians? The question was put to Descartes repeatedly – by the *Second Objector* ("an atheist knows clearly and distinctly that the three angles of a triangle are equal to two right angles" (AT 7, 125; CSM 2, 89)); by the *Fifth* ("who will believe that such atheists as Diagoras and Theodorus cannot be made completely certain by their demonstrations?" (AT 7, 328; CSM 2, 228)); by the *Sixth* ("the atheist . . . maintains that his knowledge is very certain" (AT 7, 414; CSM 2, 279)). Descartes never reversed his verdict. Of course, he held, there might occur small individual variations. An atheist might become so fluent in the proof of the three-angles theorem that he can never entertain the theorem without the proof; his knowledge will then extend to *that*. But given human mental capacity, such fluency cannot be pushed very far. To the atheist, the bulk of knowledge is a Sisyphean goal; by and large, his grasp will not rise above the level of mere conviction.

On second thoughts, Descartes probably would have said that Jason and Medea never loved each other; their feelings never rose above the level of mere fancy.

really distinct . . .

My title is a grammatical variant on two words that appear in the title of *Meditation Six*: *The existence of material things, and the real distinction between mind and body*. The variant itself occurs in the final line of a paragraph that is often taken to be the definitive formulation of Cartesian dualism – a paragraph that along with the *cogito* has made Descartes the philosopher whom we still study and remember. Here are its last few lines, call them [A]:

> The fact that I can clearly and distinctly grasp one thing apart from another is enough to make me certain that the two are distinct, since they are capable of being separated, at least by God. Simply by knowing that I exist, and observing absolutely nothing else that belongs to my nature or essence except that I am a thinking thing, I rightly conclude that my essence consists solely in the fact that I am a thinking thing. It is true that I may have (or as I shall soon say, that I certainly have) a body that is very closely joined to me. But nevertheless, on the one hand I have a clear and distinct idea of myself, in so far as I am simply a thinking, non-extended thing; and on the other hand I have a distinct idea of body, in so far as it is simply an extended, non-thinking thing. Accordingly, it is certain that I am really distinct [*revera distinctum*] from my body, and can exist without it. (*Meditation Six*: AT 7, 78; CSM 2, 54)

Descartes says in the second sentence "I rightly conclude"; so there is an argument – obviously, we shall have to examine it as well as the conclusion: they involve more technical lingo than meets the eye. But let me first draw attention to a plain yet intriguing fact.

It can be brought out most easily by setting [A] next to another text, call it [B], that we considered earlier:

> Thought – this alone is inseparable from me. *I am, I exist*, that is certain. But for how long? For as long as I think. It might perhaps even happen that if I entirely stopped thinking, I should at once altogether stop being. I admit here nothing but what is necessarily true. Strictly, then, I am only a thing that thinks, i.e. a mind, or intelligence, or intellect, or reason.

This is a post-*cogito* passage in *Meditation Two* (AT 7, 27; CSM 2, 18); you may remember I discussed it at some length in chapter 3, where it was also labeled [B]. Even at first glance, it is apparent that there are quite a few links between [A] and [B] – we shall detail them in due course. For the moment, let us simply attend to a feature that the two texts share; or if you prefer, a question that they both raise.

Start with [B], and remind yourself of the title of the *Meditation* in which it occurs: *The nature of the human mind; that it is better known than the body*. Well, if we assume that being told about what is inseparable from a thing amounts to being told about that thing's nature, then [B] does tell us about the nature of a certain thing, namely: Descartes. Final sentence of [B]: "Strictly, then, I am only a thing that thinks" – I, *ego*. On the other hand, what the title of the *Meditation* had led us to expect was a description not of the nature of Descartes, but of the nature of Descartes' *mind*. Of course one might reply that [B] is only a step toward that description. Perhaps; but as we saw when we studied *Meditation Two*, it is far from easy to tell what account it actually does give of the mind's nature. The reader has to extract it from the rather impressionistic pages that follow text [B], namely the "piece of wax." And even then, it remains a matter of speculation – [B] is what sticks in the mind as the chief lesson of *Meditation Two*.

Turn now to *Meditation Six* and look at our excerpt, also setting it beside the title. The title leads us to expect that we shall be taught about the real distinction – whatever that is – between mind and body; and yes, our text [A] does end up saying that two things are really distinct. One of them is a body: Descartes' body. So far so good. But what stands on the other side? Read the final words: "it is certain that I am really distinct from my body, and can exist without it." Again, we do not encounter what we expected: distinguished from Descartes' body is not Descartes' mind, but – Descartes. Again, "I." Now we might once more suppose that our text is only a stage in a longer journey. In fact, a few pages later (AT 7, 86; CSM 2, 59) there does come a paragraph where what is declared distinct from Descartes' body is his mind – call this text [C]:

> There is a great difference between the mind and the body, in that the body by its very nature is always divisible, while the mind is utterly indivisible. For in truth, when I consider the mind – or myself in so far as I am merely a thinking thing – I can distinguish no parts within myself; I regard myself as one and complete. . . . The faculties of willing, sensing, understanding, etc., cannot be termed parts of the mind, since it is one and the same mind that wills, senses and understands. By contrast, I can think of no corporeal or extended thing that I cannot easily divide by thought into parts, and so regard as divisible. This one fact would be enough to teach me that the mind is completely different [*omnino diversa*] from the body, even if I did not already know it well enough from other considerations.

"The mind is completely different from the body": this does accord with the *Meditation*'s title. But we might still notice that in the middle lines, at the core of the argument, "I" takes once again the place of the mind: "I can distinguish no parts within myself." And the final words – the "even-if" clause that mentions previously acquired knowledge – can only be read as a reference back to [A]. So once more, "I."

Surely, given these texts – [B] long ago, and now [A] plus [C] – the question we want to ask is: does Descartes somehow equate himself with his mind? Does he think, by contrast, that his body is only to a lesser extent him – something perhaps that he has, but isn't? Exactly what is Cartesian dualism a dualism *of*: mind and body? or self (*ego ipse*) and body? These are by no means easy questions; and a good way to begin may be to examine the arguments that Descartes offers in [A] and in [C] for the real distinction announced in the title. Let me do this, if only briefly.

From reading the *Meditations* one would not gather that "real distinction" (*realis distinctio*) is a technical phrase for Descartes. It occurs literally just once in the book – in the title of *Meditation Six*.[1] Allied adjectival forms appear twice – *revera distinctus* in our text [A], and *omnino diversa* in [C]; that is all. On the other hand we are given formal definitions in the *Replies* (AT 7, 162; CSM 2, 114) and in the *Principles*, definitions according to which there would be no real distinction between, say, *round* and *square* – for the simple reason that "round" and "square" are shapes of things, and not things themselves.[2] Real distinctions exist only between things or "substances" (*Principles*, Part 1, art. 60: AT 8a, 28; CSM 1, 213) – which shapes, of course, are not. What, then, is a substance? If we leave out God (a special case), a substance is what requires only God's concurrence in order to exist (art. 51: AT 8a, 24; CSM 1, 210): it is complete in that sense. By contrast (art. 53) a shape also requires the thing whose shape it is – roundness, for example, needs a clock or the full moon to instantiate it.

Shall we say, then, that a clock is a thing, or substance? Yes, we may – even though our village clock seems to have needed more than God's concurrence in order to exist: it took the labor of a clockmaker too, did it not? Indeed; but we might avail ourselves here of a distinction that Descartes draws, bearing on the word "body." Descartes will standardly speak of a village clock as a body (Latin: *corpus*; French: *corps*), or an extended body; but it turns out that he uses the noun in two ways. Sometimes, it is a *mass*-term – in the way "gold" is in English, or "wax."[3] There is wax in the world, of which Descartes' piece in *Meditation Two* is a fragment. Likewise there is body, *il y a du corps*. We would not, however, say in similar fashion that there is clock in the world, of which a fragment adorns the village-steeple. "Clock" to us is an *object*-noun: there are clocks in the world, among which one stands in the village square. Descartes also uses "body" in that second manner, as a word with a straight plural – there are bodies, *il y a des corps*. Come back now to the question, what counts as a substance? With a little effort of abstraction, the clock in the tower can also be viewed as a fragment of body, in the mass-sense – as a fragment of all the body there is in the universe. So viewed, it may be called a substance – derivatively, as it were. For *body*, in the mass-sense, depends only on God for its existence; and this will in turn be true of bodies in the object-sense, provided we also view them as fragments of body, taken as a mass. So while, strictly speaking, there is only one corporeal substance in the world – body – in an extended yet acceptable sense, we may call whatever we view as *a* body, a substance too.

This applies of course to one body that Descartes is particularly interested in, his own. That body is a thing, a substance. What he wishes to know is whether his mind (he?) is really distinct from it – whether his mind (he?) is a substance too, separate and complete. Our paragraphs [A] and [C] are meant as proofs that it (he?) is.

The proofs are simple. Look again at the first sentence of [A]:

> The fact that I can clearly and distinctly grasp one thing apart from another is enough to make me certain that the two are distinct, since they are capable of being separated, at least by God.

Voiced here is the principle on which the argument of [A] depends. If I can separate two things in my thought, this shows that they are really separate; they are distinct substances, God can create one without the other. But of course, it all turns on what you count as mental separation. Many people have thought separately of the Morning Star and of the Evening Star: yet these are hardly, on that account, different celestial bodies. The principle just quoted holds good only when you grasp one thing apart from another *clearly and distinctly* – which presumably untutored star-gazers do not: they have not charted any celestial orbit. So let us turn to Descartes and ask: what assures him that he sees himself, or his mind, clearly and distinctly apart from his body?

The answer goes back a long way, in fact back to *Meditation One*, where Descartes found that he could directly doubt that he had a body – he could suppose outright that God was deceiving him on that count. Under the full sway of that supposition, he was still able to engage in clear thoughts about his mind, himself, his nature: he discovered, for example, that seeing wax involved not just sensations, but an act of intellect. Does this not show that he could think of his mind apart from his body – he could reach clear conclusions about it while assuming that his body did not even exist? So, his mind is really distinct. As an aside

(Descartes himself does not use the argument), one might add that the same line of reasoning – resting on the same mental-separation principle – would show that Descartes' mind is also really distinct from other minds. Remember, while thinking about himself and the piece of wax, Descartes was also able to suppose that the men he saw through the window were mere automata, or mindless creatures. So again, he could think clearly about himself while supposing that something else did not exist – other minds. So they, too, must be distinct.

Descartes' second argument for the real distinction between mind and body (our text [C]) is less abstract, but also less convincing. It goes like this. A thing cannot have at once contrary properties; Descartes' body has parts, his mind has not; so the two are perforce distinct. Let us not question the contrary-properties principle, though one certainly could – it underestimates, for example, the possibility of there being different *perspectives* on the same object. My naive eyes see the sun as rising and setting; my tutored ones, as a motionless celestial body; the same sun I see, then, at once immobile and moving. Even if we disallow this sort of counter-example and insist on strict vision, we are bound to feel uneasy about another premise of the argument, the one about the mind or self having no parts. Isn't "part of me" a standard locution to report mental conflicts? Part of me trembles at the thought of scaling the North Face of the Eiger, yet I am dying to try. Ah, Descartes will reply, this is not a mental conflict. The phrase is a misnomer, there can be no such thing: for a conflict to arise there must be parties, and the mind has none. What is really happening here is a conflict between my mind on one side, and a bodily impulse on the other – so Descartes will argue at length in article 47 of the *Passions* (AT 11, 364–6; CSM 1, 345–7). But this view is not very convincing. My predicament re the North Face does not feel at all like a typical conflict between mind and body – say, my wish to stifle a sneeze during a concert. It feels mental all round. Descartes' blunt denial that it is, his blunt insistence that the mind has no parts, require more support than they receive in *Meditation Six* – or for that matter elsewhere in his work. To that extent, the second argument for real distinction (i.e., our text [C]) requires more support, too.

Still, [C] is only an adjunct, as Descartes makes quite clear: the master beam is [A], and so we should look at it a bit further. Perhaps a good way to begin is to consider the assessment that Arnauld – a well-disposed reader – offered after having examined [A] in detail, in the *Fourth* set of *Objections* (AT 7, 203; CSM 2, 143). He writes this:

> It looks as though the argument proves too much and takes us back to the Platonic view (which the author nonetheless rejects) that nothing corporeal belongs to our essence, so that man is merely a soul, and the body

merely a vehicle of the soul – a view which gives rise to the definition of man as "a soul that makes use of a body."

I shall deal later with the view that the argument "proves too much" – a very prophetic insight, as we shall see. For the moment, let us just consider the charge that the argument leads to the conclusion that man is a soul or mind that "makes use of a body."

First, the equation of man with mind or soul: even the text is instructive on that count. Look again at the conclusion of [A], as it appears in *Meditation Six*:

> it is certain that I am really distinct from my body, and can exist without it.

In his *Second Reply* (AT 7, 132; CSM 2, 95) Descartes quotes that sentence to his *objectors* – like this:

> it is certain that I (*i.e. the mind*) am really distinct from my body, and can exist without it. [The italics are in the text]

When the French version of the *Reply* came out a few years later, even more words were added (I translate):

> it is certain that I, i.e. my mind or soul through which I am what I am, is really distinct from my body, and can exist without it.

Moi, mon esprit, mon âme: in case the readers of *Meditation Six* had not got the equation clear, here it is, spelled out by Descartes as he (mis?)quotes himself. What is more, *Meditation Six*, as now amended, is almost a straight echo of *Meditation Two* – look back to [B]: "strictly, I am only a thing that thinks, i.e. a mind, or intelligence, or intellect, or reason." Granted, in [B] the equation was presented as provisional, for at that stage Descartes was in the grips of the doubt, he was supposing that perhaps he had no body at all – God might be deceiving him on that score. But those days are gone. God is no deceiver; in fact, as Descartes is about to show, God's integrity guarantees that Descartes has a body (see [A]: "I shall soon say, I certainly have a body"). So [A]'s conclusion – the identification of himself with his mind or soul, the separation of himself from his body – cannot be viewed as a transitional move: it is the final word.[4]

Little wonder, then, that Arnauld should read [A] as showing that the mind "makes use of the body"; or that another reader, Regius, should take himself to be propounding straight Cartesian doctrine when he declares that human creatures are mere beings "*per accidens.*"[5] My body is just something that I happen to have, it is "really distinct" from what I am (look at the last quote from Descartes, above). I might have had a different body; I might even have had no body at all – "my soul would still be all that it is, even if my body did not exist" (*Discourse*, Part 4: AT 6, 33; CSM 1, 127). Nor is it a surprise that the view that my mind makes me what I am should cohere with the doctrine that we saw could be extracted from "the piece of wax" – that there is no thought without thought of oneself. If my mind is *me*, is it not quite plausible that any thinking I do, any consciousness I have, should carry with it the thought of myself? On this count too, *Meditation Six* presents a view similar to the one we were offered in *Meditation Two*.

What, then, is in our sights now? What exactly is involved in the fact that my mind or soul is distinct from my body?

First of all, the soul is not what gives life to the body:

> Death never occurs through the absence of the soul, but only because one of the main parts of the body decays. The difference between the body of a living man and that of a dead man is just like the difference between a watch or other automaton (i.e., a self-moving machine) when it is wound up and contains in itself the corporeal principle of the movements for which it is designed, together with everything else required for its operation; and on the other hand, the same watch when it is broken and the principle of the movement ceases to be active.

This statement, incidentally, occurs not in our *Meditation*, but in Descartes' final published work, the *Passions of the Soul* (art. 6: AT 11, 330–1; CSM 1, 329–30).

In fact my body *is* like a watch or a clock:

> I do not recognize any difference between artifacts and natural bodies except that the operations of artifacts are for the most part performed by mechanisms that are large enough to be easily perceivable by the senses – as indeed they must be if they are capable of being manufactured by human beings. The effects produced in nature, by contrast, always depend on structures that are so minute that they completely elude our sense. . . . It is no less natural for a clock constructed with this or that set of wheels to tell the time than it is for a tree that grew from this or that seed to produce the appropriate fruit.

Again, this is not in the *Meditations*, but in that later work which Descartes intended as a textbook, the *Principles* (Part 4, art. 203: AT 8a, 326; CSM 1, 288).

What else? Well, take an example. Suppose that I am at this moment scaling the North Face; and as I do, I spot the nearest cleft in the rock, and wedge my left foot into it. According to Cartesian doctrine, at least three episodes have occurred in this segment of my climb: first a train of internal bodily motions, from eye to brain; then a non-bodily, mental train – my seeing and deciding; and then another train of bodily motions, from brain to foot. As far as episodes *one* and *three* of this sequence go, everything is mechanical; nothing happens different in kind from what would happen in a functioning clock – wheels turning, levers rising, cords being pulled, etc., etc. Descartes spent years dissecting dogs, to discover exactly what those body-mechanisms were: he describes them in various technical writings, and even alludes to them briefly in *Meditation Six* (AT 7, 86; CSM 2, 59–60). As it happens, posterity has not concurred with the detail of these findings; but philosophically that is no great matter. What *has* preoccupied philosophers is the middle episode of my tale – the non-bodily train that has supposedly taken place between the two sets of mechanical moves. For it does raise important questions.

First of all, must it exist in the way that Descartes describes it? Don't forget that, for him, the thoughts that I have just had – my seeing the rock-cleft, my perhaps pondering, my deciding to move the foot – are all events that took place in my mind; nothing corresponding to them need have happened in the brain, or elsewhere in the body. My thoughts occurred independently, they were modes of a distinct substance – *that* is what Descartes takes the import of the proof of "real distinction" to be, the import of our text [A]. And of course, we might well wonder whether so much does follow from the simple proof that mind and body are "capable of being separated, at least by God" (see the first sentence of [A]). Does it really follow, from that simple proof, that I am not a fully material creature – that what I did on the rock-face cannot be fully accounted for by events in my body and in my brain? As the *Sixth Objectors* asked (AT 7, 413; CSM 2, 278), "is it self-contradictory that our thoughts should be reducible to these corporeal motions?"

Something else bothered seventeenth-century readers of the *Meditations* it seems even more. I have just spoken of thoughts occurring *independently* of the body; but according to Descartes, in some cases they do not. As *he* would describe the events of my example, the middle episode in my bit of climb – the mental one, the sequence of my seeing, deliberating and deciding – was initiated by something happening during the earlier, bodily, episode: it was initiated by the motion of one small part of my brain, "the part which is said to contain the common sense" (*Meditation Six*: AT 7, 86; CSM 2, 59); "common", here, presumably meaning "common to mind and brain." Descartes usually calls that brain-part the *conarion*, or *petite glande*:[6] a specific motion of the *petite glande*, then, is what caused me to see the cleft. And conversely, episode three – the body sequence that issued in the motion of my foot – also began with a motion of the little gland; but this time, a motion

really distinct . . .

caused by a *mental* event, namely, the decision which I had made. So it turns out that mind and body can "act on one another" – that is Descartes' phrase, for example in the *Passions* (art. 34: AT 11, 354; CSM 1, 341); they can act via the gland. In that sense – again *Passions* (art. 32) – the *petite glande* is said to be the "principal seat" of the soul, or mind.[7]

Let us leave aside the problem of there being just one seat – just one spot in the brain where mind and body could interact; Descartes offered this as a mere conjecture anyway (again article 32). What preoccupied his readers much more was that there should be any seat at all. For example, Gassendi asked: "How can the soul, if it is in no way material, move the body; and how can it receive the forms of corporeal objects?" (*Appendix* to *Fifth Objections and Replies*, AT 9a, 213; CSM 2, 275). Princess Elisabeth asked likewise – indeed, that is the question with which their correspondence began (May 16, 1643; AT 3, 661). After Descartes' long and prompt reply, she begged that her "stupidity be excused": she was still "unable to understand how one could hold that the soul (inextended and immaterial) could move the body" (June 20, 1643; AT 3, 684).

What was Descartes' answer? Or rather, what were they? – there is a range of them. To Gassendi, a not greatly liked questioner, Descartes replied like this:

[T]he most ignorant can, in a quarter of an hour, raise more such questions than the wisest can deal with in a lifetime; so I have not bothered to answer any of them. . . . I shall merely say that the entire problem arises from a supposition that is false and can in no way be proved – that if the soul and the body are two substances whose nature is different, this prevents them from being able to act on one another. (*Appendix*: AT 9a, 213; CSM 2, 275)

To the Princess, the tone is somewhat different:

I may truly say that the question which Your Highness poses seems to me the one which can most properly be put to me in view of my published writings.

In fact this letter (May 21 1643; AT 3, 663–8; CSMK 217–20), plus the next one he wrote to Elisabeth a month later, on June 28 (AT 3, 690–5; CSMK, 226–9) in answer to her confession of "stupidity", are probably the most oft-printed items in Descartes' correspondence; they are lively and direct; they foster discussion even today.[8]

The reason why he omitted in the *Meditations* all talk of interaction between mind and body, Descartes tells the Princess, is that it would have undermined his principal aim, which was to prove their distinction. Undermined, how so? For an answer, let us first look at a text to which Descartes directs Elisabeth – the last section of his *Reply* to the *Sixth* set of *Objections*.

It is an eight-page piece of intellectual autobiography (AT 7, 439–47; CSM 2, 296–301), where Descartes begins by recounting how, even after he had conclusively proved that his mind and body were distinct substances, he was still not fully convinced: "I was in the same plight as astronomers who have established by argument that the sun is several times larger than the earth, and still cannot prevent themselves judging that it is smaller, when they look at it" (440). Why the vacillation? It had its roots in a prejudice acquired during childhood.[9] Children, Descartes thinks, are unable to rely on mere intellect; they depend on sense and imagination for all their ideas and, consequently, "there is nothing which [they] do not take to be corporeal" (441). What is more, that prejudice is only too apt to survive into adult life: we are forever ready to regress into the materialism of our childhood – this is what happened to Descartes after his proof. To thwart a similar lapse among his readers is why Descartes omitted to discuss interaction and focused on distinction, i.e. concentrated on proving that the mind was a substance distinct from the body – *that* being the much harder task, since it went against the infantile materialism on which many would still be fixated.

Let me now return to the letters. There, Descartes offers an even stronger reason why he did not talk about interaction in the *Meditations*, namely this. To think that the mind can move the body, and vice versa, is to hold that there is a *union* of them (May 21, 1643, *letter*: AT 3, 665; CSMK, 218). Nor is Descartes using that word in some weak sense, to mean perhaps not much more than "interaction" – which, incidentally, is a word that he *never* uses. No: in the June letter he tells the Princess that in order to have the idea of the union of mind and body, "one must conceive them as a single thing" (*il faut les concevoir comme une seule chose*). Hence, it is quasi-impossible to think jointly of distinction and of union, for this would amount to jointly thinking of body and mind as two, and as one – "which is absurd" (AT 3, 693; CSMK, 227). Small wonder, then, that when he sought to demonstrate distinction, Descartes left interaction undiscussed.

What is the upshot? It is clear that the thought Descartes wants above all to convey to the Princess is that the less we try to analyze or even reflect on mind–body interaction, the better. Interaction is a primitive, underived notion; it "can be understood only through itself" (May *letter*: AT 3, 666; CSMK, 218); and "people who never philosophize and use only their senses, have no doubt that the soul moves the body and that the body acts on the soul" (June *letter*: AT 3, 692; CSMK, 227). In fact – and here Descartes begs the Princess to take his words seriously – he himself has never spent more than "a few hours a year" on thoughts that occupied only the intellect.

The Princess got the message and never asked about mind and body again. More distant readers of Descartes, however, might well be moved to some reflexions – here are two or three.

We might first observe that in the published writings that followed the May and June 1643 letters – namely, the *Principles* in 1644, and the *Passions* in 1649 – even though he continued to propound the doctrine of interaction, Descartes did not depart from the laconicism that he had counseled to the Princess. He continued to speak of soul and body *acting on one another* (see title of art. 34 of the *Passions* – AT 11, 354; CSM 1, 341); of the soul having its *principal seat* in the brain (see art. 189 of Part 4 of the *Principles* – AT 8a, 315–16; CSM 1, 279–80; also the *Passions*, title of art. 32 – AT 11, 352; CSM 1, 340); of the soul or mind being *intimately joined* to the brain (art. 189 of Part 4 of the *Principles*; also art. 190), or even *being in* the brain (art. 196). But he never elaborated in any way on any of these formulas.[10] The qualms that Gassendi and Elisabeth had voiced were never even alluded to – the doctrine of primitive notion ruled the roost.

It did not, however, govern the thoughts of the seventeenth-century post-Cartesian philosophers whom we still read today: Spinoza, Malebranche, or Leibniz. Mind–body dualists they remained, in one way or another; but they all turned their back on interaction and held something else in their sights, the most striking landscape being Leibniz's grand expanse of *pre-established harmony*. Think again of the North Face, of my sighting a cleft and securing a foot into it. This wasn't my mind causing my body to move, as the interactionist confusedly believes. No: these were two clocks ringing at the same time, my mind deciding and my foot moving – two clocks that had, since time began, been set (Leibniz says "pre-established"; we might say "programmed") to ring in unison. How would Descartes have reacted to this depiction? Would he have retorted that he found no notion of mind–body harmony in his stock of primitive ideas? Would we find such a retort convincing? Who knows?

Let me make one final remark about Cartesian interaction, starting from the abrupt answer to Gassendi that I quoted a few pages ago. Disregard the dig about ignorance and concentrate on the final lines – Descartes' diagnosis that objections to interaction arise from the false supposition that "if the soul and the body are two substances whose nature is different, this prevents them from being able to act on one another" (AT 9a, 213; CSM 2, 275). Ask yourself, independently of Descartes, why do *anti*-interactionists think as they do? One answer might be that they think in a certain manner about causation. As perhaps many people do (whether consciously or not), they might think of it as involving some sort of *flow*, a stream flowing from the cause to the effect. On that view, if my decision caused the motion of my foot, some current must have flowed from my mind to (first) the gland, making the gland move. Well, if *this* needs to have happened for my mind to have acted on my body, might we not easily find ourselves in Gassendi's and Elisabeth's camp – unable to grasp how it could have happened at all? unable to grasp how a flux coming from the mind – a spiritual or ethereal flux – could have moved a material object like a gland, no matter how "little" that gland was? So the charge that mind–body interaction is really unintelligible might well depend on our having a certain conception of causation – call it a *flux*-conception. And it might be that Descartes' counter-charge is really an attack on that conception, declaring it unnecessary or even incoherent. It might be. Given his terseness, though, this is no more than a conjecture.

Let us pause and look back. In the created world, according to the view that has emerged so far, there are minds and there is body. One of these minds is *me*; and what I call *my* body is that fragment of the total world-body with which my mind interacts. *My* eyes, for example, are those two globes that directly face the rock-cleft which I now see; and *my* foot is that end of limb which will lodge itself into the cleft when I decide to move. I might have had a different body, perhaps even no body at all: in that sense, we might concur with Regius' formula, which he took to be Cartesian, that a human creature is an *ens per accidens* – an "accidental being." And we might also concur with Arnauld's assessment which I quoted earlier (see pp. 107–8) – that the *Meditation Six* argument for real distinction amounts to defining man as "a soul that makes use of a body." My body enables me to feel (excitedly) anxious as I now climb, and filled with pride later, when I stand at the top.

However – however – that is not the whole story, as Arnauld also pointed out in our passage, when he said that the argument "proved too much." I take this phrase to mean that the argument led to a conclusion that was not really Descartes'. In his reply, Descartes certainly insists that "soul-making-use-of-the-body" is *not* what he has argued (AT 7, 228; CSM 2, 160):

> I thought I was very careful against anyone inferring that man was simply "a soul that makes use of a body." For in the *Sixth Meditation*, where I dealt with the distinction between mind and body, I also proved that the mind is substantially united [*substantialiter unitam*] with the body; and the arguments which I used are as strong as any I can remember ever having read anywhere else.

As for the statement that "man is a being *per accidens*," Descartes' response was that he (Regius) "could scarcely have said anything more objectionable and provocative" (*letter* to Regius, December 1641: AT 3,

460; CSMK, 200) – a definite enough answer. So we should ask ourselves: exactly what, beside distinction and interaction, does Descartes take himself to have shown?

The answer is by no means easy. It turns on nine difficult pages (AT 7, 81–9; CSM 2, 56–61) of the second half of *Meditation Six*; and on echoes of them, elsewhere in the corpus.[11] First, we find a new vocabulary – most strikingly, perhaps, the two words that we have just met in the lines where Descartes tells Arnauld what he has proved: that his mind and his body are *substantially united*. That phrase does not actually occur in the *Meditation*, but some cousins do. Descartes, we are told (81), is "quasi-intermingled" (*quasi permixtus*) with his body; his mind and body make up a "composite" (*compositum*) (82, 83, 85) – terms that are clearly meant to convey the idea of a tie stronger than mere interaction. My being "quasi-intermingled" with my body amounts to something more than my having the power to act on it, and vice versa. The question is, what?

To begin with, it means that we should look upon our sensations in a new way: "sensory perceptions were given to me by nature merely to inform the mind of what is beneficial or harmful for the composite of which the mind is a part" (AT 7, 83; CSM 2, 57). Contrast this with *Meditation Two* (AT 7, 28; CSM 2, 19). There, you may remember, sensations were also mentioned; but they were mentioned simply as *thoughts* – thoughts that a perhaps-disembodied Descartes was having. Angels might have them too. But now, further up the path, we can see that this was a narrow and limited landscape: only a "composite" creature, a creature composed of mind-plus-body, will have the sensations that we have, since their sole and proper function is to inform that creature about what is beneficial or harmful to it. "If an angel were in a human body, he would not have sensations as we do, but would simply perceive the motions that are caused by external objects, and in this way would differ from a real human" (*letter* to Regius, January 1642: AT 3, 493; CSMK 206).[12]

Nor is it just a matter of what angels feel. Descartes will also draw more earthly conclusions from the fact that our senses have only a preservative function. For one thing, it means that they need not give us correct information about what things are really like: "I misuse [my sensations] by treating them as reliable touchstones for immediate judgments about the essential nature of bodies located outside us" (AT 7, 83; CSM 2, 57–8). The clock-face that I see as round may actually be round; but other perceptions are not like that. Distant stars look small, expanses where I see nothing look empty: but in neither case do the looks mirror reality. Nor are they likely to mirror it when I see green grass or feel heat from a fire: of course, *something* is present in the grass and in the fire; but nothing that need in any way resembles what I see or feel.

Descartes nowhere tells his readers how perceiving, say, greenness in a blade of grass is more apt to inform us about what is beneficial for the mind–body complex than perceiving waves-and-particles would have been; but we can imagine what he might say. More interesting is the fact that in a later work, the *Passions*, he will extend this functionalist outlook to another segment of our mental life, namely our feelings and emotions – his term is "passions":

> [T]he function of all the passions consists solely in this, that they dispose our soul to want the things that nature deems useful for us, and to persist in this volition. (Art. 52: AT 11, 372; CSM 1, 349)

Nor are these mere abstract words. They will force Descartes to deny the status of feeling to, for example, *cruelty* (art. 207) – no usefulness is detectable here. And conversely, they will force him to argue for the usefulness of *jealousy* (art. 168) – which is a feeling, without a doubt. Of course jealousy is not always proper (*honnête*): "a captain defending a very important position has the right to be jealous of it"; but "we have contempt for a man who is jealous of his wife" (169). Like all feelings, jealousy has its pathology: it can be abnormal or exaggerated or misplaced. And this brings us back to *Meditation Six* – because much of its difficult last pages, the pages about the quasi-intermingling or substantial union of mind and body, is taken up with the discussion of one case of *abnormal* sensation. We should look at it a bit more closely, because, as usual with Descartes, the study of abnormality is meant to teach us what normality is like.

Consider a man suffering from dropsy – a sickness that makes him want to drink even though his body is already saturated with water: something is not working right. The question is, exactly what do we mean when we speak of malfunction here? Let us compare with my example of long ago, the village-clock whose bell rings haphazardly – sometimes four chimes, say, at three o'clock. Here, too, we have a malfunction; but again in what sense, exactly? We cannot be thinking of the clock taken just by itself: "a clock constructed with wheels and weights observes all the laws of nature just as closely when it is badly made and tells the wrong time, as when it fully fulfills the wishes of the clockmaker" (AT 7, 84; CSM 2, 58). Likewise, the dropsical man's body observes the laws of physiology no less than the healthy man's. With the clock, however, there is no problem explaining why we say that it does not work properly: it does not fulfill the *function* for which it was built – a clock is supposed to ring three, not four, times when the hands indicate three o'clock. In Descartes' idiom, we might say that our clock is "departing from its nature" – the noun "nature," here, being "a label dependent on my thoughts and extraneous to the thing to which it is applied" (85). Had it been built for a different purpose – say, to keep blind villagers guessing – our clock would not be departing from its nature when it rings as it does.

Well, can we not say likewise that the dropsical man's body is departing from its nature, when his throat is dry even though his body is logged with fluid? Yes, we can; but – and this is Descartes' crucial thesis – we are now speaking differently. We are no longer using the word "nature" as an extraneous label; we are not saying that something is happening in a piece of mechanism, contrary to the wishes of its maker. No, there is now a "true error of nature": a certain entity is being harmed, or damaged. What entity? It can only be the mind–body complex that the dropsical man consists in. So the conclusion we must draw from the example of dropsy is that a certain category of descriptions – those relating to the malfunction or abnormality of a human organ: "his sense of when to drink is undermined by his illness", "her eyes aren't working properly" – makes sense only on the supposition that we are talking about a mind–body complex, a mind intermingled with a body; or, to use the phrase from the *Reply* to Arnauld, a mind substantially united to a body. And of course, what applies to abnormality also applies to its opposite: "her eyes are fine" carries the same presupposition. So an entire idiom about human beings carries the implication that they are not just a mind and a body acting on one another, but a mind and a body joined together much more tightly.

As we saw, in his *Reply* to Arnauld, Descartes writes that his arguments for substantial union are "as strong as any [he] remembers ever having read anywhere" (AT 7, 228; CSM 2, 160). Perhaps; yet they have not been strong enough. It isn't that posterity has found fault and criticized; rather, it has ignored. The arguments interest Cartesian scholars, of course;[13] but they are not features of what philosophical tradition regards as Cartesianism. Arnauld was only too prescient when he warned that the demonstration of mind–body distinction "proved too much": it is as though Descartes' readers stopped reading and closed the book once argument [A] was offered. Who knows, they were perhaps also hearing Descartes' other voice – the one he professes to the Princess to have used when he tells her in the May letter that he played down mind–body union in the *Meditations* so as to convince readers of the opposite, namely their distinction. The underplay has worked very well, for centuries now.

What have later generations, then, retained of *Meditation Six*? First and foremost are our texts [A] and [C] – the demonstration that we are not merely particles of matter, but creatures made up of two substances, one of them immaterial. In Descartes' eyes, this is the crucial step forward from *Meditation Two*: there, not knowing whether he had a body at all, he had been able to affirm that he was a thinking thing; but "might it not be that these very things which I am supposing to be nothing because they are unknown to me, are in reality identical with the 'I' of which I am aware? I do not know" (AT 7, 27; CSM 2, 18). Well, *that* possibility has now been dismissed; he has escaped the fear that everything should amount to plain matter. Whether more of the afterglow of the earlier *Meditation* remains, whether Descartes still identifies himself with his mind, is not easy to tell. As we saw, many of his pronouncements would suggest that he does – Arnauld has not been alone in reading the lines that way.

Posterity also remembers the doctrine of interaction via the little gland, even though in our *Meditation* it receives only a very brief mention ("countless observations establish it, which there is no need to review here": AT 7, 86; CSM 2, 59); and it also remembers the equation of the human body with a clock, although it, too, is spoken of only on one page – and hypothetically: "if I consider the body of man as a sort of machine . . ." (84). Obviously, other works of Descartes – plus the correspondence, especially the May and June 1643 letters to Elisabeth – have carried weight here.

What view of the mind tradition has been ascribed to Descartes, I shall discuss in the next chapter. I want to end the present one by looking again at what we gazed at when we began our trek through the *Meditations* – the tangled scenery of trust, distrust, and deceit.

It will probably come as no surprise that thoughts of deceit should be much present in the *Sixth Meditation*. They are. For example we are told that nature deceives the dropsical man; and Descartes will devote the terminal pages of the *Meditation* (85–9) to explaining how that happens, and how it nonetheless does not incriminate God – it does not follow that God is himself a deceiver. And deceit, or rather non-deceit, will also have played a decisive role a few pages earlier (79–80), in the proof that material objects exist: don't forget, this is one of the aims of the final *Meditation*, as announced in its title.

The proof is extremely simple. Descartes has a great inclination (*magnam propensionem*) to believe that his ideas of material objects, or bodies, really come from material bodies. What is more, that inclination is part of his native make-up, it has been lodged into him by God; and his belief, if it turned out to be mistaken, could never be corrected – for God has given him no means to discover such a mistake. So: "I do not see how God could be understood not to be a deceiver if these ideas were transmitted from a source other than corporeal things. It follows that

really distinct . . .

corporeal things exist" (80). QED. It is safe to conjecture that this proof has not made many converts – most skeptics finding it easier to believe in an external world than to believe in God; and therefore more inclined, if at all, to envisage a journey of discovery from the world to God, than the other way round. But the proof has also elicited a much more corrosive objection.

Leibniz, I think, was the first to voice it:

> There would be no deception of rational creatures even if everything outside them did not correspond exactly to their experiences, or indeed if nothing did – say, if there was only one mind. Everything would happen just as if all other things existed, and this mind – acting rationally – could not complain of having been wronged. For to be in *that* state, is not to be deceived.

This is a letter that Leibniz wrote toward the end of his life, in 1715, three-quarters of a century after the *Meditations*.[14] The objection is terse, but far-reaching: one might embroider it like this.

If God made us believe what was false, we can fairly assume that it would be forever; we should never find out. Now, looking at the scene from the standpoint of the dupe, we must surely come to the conclusion that this is no deceit at all. There can be neither discovery nor the pain that attends it; no fear, therefore, of that pain; no suspicion or, oppositely, relief; no distrust or, oppositely, trust. It seems that no toe-hold remains for *any* of the thoughts or feelings or attitudes that surround our ordinary experience of having been lied to, or taken in. What sense, then, remains in speaking of deceit? Of course, you might insist that it is still there – in some absolute manner of speaking. But the insistence rings pretty hollow. Leibniz, again: "to be in that state, is not to be deceived."

This is of course a devastating charge. So, far from being "hyperbolic," it says, Descartes' worry about a deceiving God is whimsical and vacuous; vacuous too, its dismissal in *Meditation Four*; and equally vacuous, the *Meditation Six* proof which relies on that dismissal. As far as I can tell, the charge has only had a sporadic life. But interestingly, it was voiced again with great power, a generation or two ago, thanks to Wittgenstein's insistence that concepts have meaning only within a context – and there is none available for the doubt of the deceiving God.[15]

What to say? Let me just hazard two comments. First, about Descartes: he certainly did hold that if, contrary to our beliefs, there happened to be no material world at all, we would never find out – "God has given me no faculty whatsoever for recognizing any [other] source for these ideas" (79–80). The dupery would be eternal. And he also held that this would make the dupery graver, not slighter: what acquits God of the charge of deceiving, for example, the dropsical man is the fact that the man's misguided thirst is not "a falsity in [his] opinions that cannot be corrected by some other faculty given [him] by God" (80) – the man can discover easily enough that he shouldn't drink whenever he feels thirsty. On the other hand, if we – human beings – believed falsely in the existence of a material world, no similar plea could be entered on God's behalf. We would not be disabused, ever; God would be a deceiver, period.

So Descartes is fair game for Leibniz's and Wittgenstein's attack. Must he succumb? Surely, a few things can be said on his side. To begin with, isn't it true that the contextualist story looks much more plausible when the false belief (as the absolutist would call it) makes the believer *better off*? – that is, when the fostering of that belief would be called *benevolent* deceit, were it called deceit? Consider a contrary situation: Plato's marriage lottery. The ideal state, Plato holds, depends on eugenics – it is important that the best beget the best; therefore, the rulers must ensure that the less-than-perfect guardians are always assigned less-than-perfect mates (the best mates being reserved for the best guardians). However, to prevent anger and resentment, the assignment is officially made through a lottery – rigged, of course (*Republic*, Bk 5, 460a). Let me add an extra feature, to make the parallel with God's deceit closer – let us suppose that, apart from the ruler, nobody can ever find out: nobody, ever. Question: would we still be willing to entertain the suggestion that the guardians who keep drawing a less-than-perfect mate are *not* being deceived? Not for an instant, I believe.

We would of course have one further reason for our reluctance: in the situation as described, one person after all *does* know about the rigging – namely, the ruler. Think of all the trappings that deceit involves, on the deceiver's side – endeavor, scheming, fear of discovery, cover-ups. Granted, none of these would apply to a deceiving God; he is above them. But there would still be his knowledge of our (false) beliefs, and the distancing that it involved. What would it be like for God if he gave us all these beliefs about skies and roses and loving friends, and none were true? Of course we can dismiss that question, too, by arguing that it over-personalizes God: such would doubtless be Leibniz's bent.[16] But we should remember that it is not Descartes'; or at least, it often is not – remember how he pictures God as a craftsman.

To conclude, then: the lures of the Leibniz–Wittgenstein paradox are poised on a razor's edge, and extra weight needs to be added to one side, to keep the whole conceit from crashing – a weight which Descartes may well refuse to add. So he probably does survive the objection.

really distinct . . .

self-esteem

A few years ago a book came out, with the challenging title: *Descartes' Error*.[1] It was not especially about Descartes – in fact, only five pages dealt with the philosopher's actual words. What concerned the author, Antonio Damasio, was the impact that "Cartesianism" (my quotation marks are deliberate) had for the past few centuries had on biological and medical research. The Cartesian divide between mind and body – and here Damasio quotes the *Discourse* passage that we met in the last chapter, about my mind remaining "all that it is, even if my body did not exist" – has until very recently led biologists and medical scientists to concentrate exclusively on the body, and to ignore the mind. And it has also led them to set a chasm between intellect and the emotions: here Damasio does not quote any text, but he could easily have pointed to the lines of *Meditation Two* where Descartes declares that he is only "a mind or intelligence or intellect or reason." Centuries of Descartes-induced misperception and myopia, Damasio thinks, have left deep marks – among them, the favor enjoyed by so-called "alternative" medicine (257). And they are only beginning to be erased by recent work in neuro-physiology – work that he, a neuro-scientist, describes in detail in the bulk of the book.

Shades of Arnauld! Would he not see here but another confirmation of his verdict that Descartes had proved too much? We read in Damasio of the "abyssal separation" between mind and body that our philosopher has promoted (249); of the "pride and joy" that Descartes feels whenever we suppress our emotions (171). Nor is Damasio alone; such labels are often pegged on Descartes – just recall the tag affixed on mainstream medicine by the advocates of holistic therapy. Whether he deserves them is, of course, another matter. We saw in the last chapter how he reacted to the first; let me now devote some space to discussing the second – the disdain of emotions.

You may remember that when I first considered the *cogito* I wondered why it had, ever since it saw the light of day, invited such massive spoofing: *I shop therefore I am, I run therefore I am, I email therefore I am* – the list is endless. And I conjectured that the parodies probably carried one common note, they rang a chime of protest against the exclusionary outlook that the *cogito* seemed to embody: "intellect, Descartes was heard as saying, is what makes me properly human – not feelings or emotions or desires." Nor would that reaction be weakened by one's encountering, a bare two pages after the adage, the line that I have quoted so many times: "strictly, then, I am only a thing that thinks, i.e. a mind, or intelligence, or intellect, or reason" (AT 7, 27; CSM 2, 18).

Now, true enough, the reader is soon told that this is only an interim description – Descartes is supposing that he might not have a body at all (hence the "strictly"). True also, in the page that immediately follows, feelings *are* added to the list of thoughts; and this is repeated at the beginning of the next *Meditation*. True, indeed. Yet, in those lists, feelings always come last – almost as an afterthought, it seems; and ten pages into that *Third Meditation*, we are further told that some (many? all? – it is unclear) of our sensations have this feature: they present as *something* what is in fact *nothing* (AT 7, 43; CSM 2, 30). So: senses, feelings, desires, emotions, even if they are thoughts, only seem to rate as second-class ones.

That was *Meditation Two*; it is astounding what spell it continues to cast! Yet have we not climbed higher – to the far summit of *Meditation Six* in fact, a crest from which broader vistas are in sight, and affairs of the heart do not look so puny in the life of the mind?

> Let me tell you that in examining the passions I have found almost all of them to be good, and to be so useful to this life that our soul would have no reason to wish to remain joined to its body even for one instant, if it could not feel them.

These words are not in the *Meditations*, but in a letter to Chanut written a few years afterwards (November 1, 1646: AT 4, 538; CSMK, 300). And they are perhaps even topped by the title of the final article of the *Passions* – as it turns out, the last lines of philosophy that Descartes was ever to write: "It is on the passions alone that all the good and evil of this life depends" (AT 11, 488; CSM 1, 404). Measure how far we have traveled from the intellectual monastery of *Meditation Two* – a journey already announced, we saw, in the final pages of the *Meditations*. And with it, another exodus may have taken place, also away from official Cartesianism – in this instance, away from the equation of thought with consciousness.

Texts surrounding the *Meditations* were of course quite rigid on the equation side. "We cannot have any thought of which we are not conscious the very moment that it is in us," said the *Reply* to Arnauld (*Fourth* set of *Replies*: AT 7, 246; CSM 2, 171); and this only echoed in a definition given two *Replies* earlier (*Second* set: AT 7, 160; CSM 2, 113):

"I use the term *thought* to include everything that is in us in such a way that we are immediately conscious (*immediate conscii*) of it." By this test, boredom, for example, is a typical thought – a state of which its owner is immediately aware: if I feel bored, I *am* bored; and if I feel not, I am not.

The equation between *mental* and *conscious* is often viewed as one of Descartes' chief legacies. Three centuries or so later, Freud, for example, will complain that "we look upon consciousness as nothing more nor less than the *defining* characteristic of the mental. . . . Indeed it seems to us so much a matter of course to equate them that any contradiction of this idea strikes us as obvious nonsense." Freud is of course exaggerating – he is not such a lone heretic: ever since Leibniz, there has existed a lineage of dissent from the Cartesian equation.[2] Let me ask a textual question, though: is the equation even wholeheartedly Cartesian? does he always stick to it?

First a general remark. The more we confine ourselves to considering just abstract and deliberative thought, the more likely we are to insist on a close link between thought and consciousness. "He is mulling over where to invest in the stock-market" *of course* implies that he is aware of what he is doing – one would be hard put to construct a scenario where such mulling occurred unknown to oneself. On the other hand, the less we have in mind that sort of cogitation, i.e. the more we turn to feelings, moods and emotions, the more inclined we shall be to challenge the thought-consciousness equation – whether this be (like Freud) at a theoretical level or in the examples that we discuss. Read this:

> When a husband mourns his departed wife – whom (as sometimes happens) he would be sorry to see brought back to life again – it may be that his heart is wrung by the sadness aroused in him by the funeral display and by the absence of a person to whose conversation he was accustomed; and it may be that some remnants of love or pity, present in his imagination, draw genuine tears from his eyes. Nonetheless he at the same time feels a secret joy in his innermost soul, and this emotion has so much power that the sadness (and the tears that go with it) can do nothing to diminish its force.

A tangled tale, isn't it? and yes, the author is Descartes (*Passions*, article 147: AT 11, 441; CSM 1, 381). As we read, we must surely wonder about the secret joy (*joie secrète*) that the husband is said to feel in his innermost soul (*dans le plus intérieur de son âme*): in what sense, exactly, is it secret? just from other mourners? or from himself too? Our text does not tell; yet somehow it is difficult to believe that Descartes would at once disallow the more inclusive interpretation and insist that if the husband has joy, then he is bound to know it. For one thing, earlier in the book (article 28: AT 11, 349–50; CSM 1, 339) he has pointed out that "those who are most agitated by their passions are not the ones who know them best": might not our husband be agitated in just that way? We might also wish to ask about the "innermost soul" where the joy is said to be located – exactly what makes it innermost? Might not interiority, here, mean distance from, perhaps even opacity to, consciousness? Odds are that it does. Incidentally, we might also ask how this idiom of "innermost soul" squares with the insistence, in the argument for mind–body distinction that we met in the last chapter, that, in contrast with the body, the soul had no parts. Granted, the phrase is a metaphor; but it remains that the metaphor comes easily enough, even to Descartes' pen.

Does this mean, then, that in the 1640s Descartes changed his mind? Perhaps; but we might also imagine a less drastic scenario. We might liken Descartes to the husband of his story. On the one hand, officially, so to speak, he identifies thought and consciousness – these are our texts from the *Replies*. But another side is ready to accommodate anomalies or exceptions. Just as the tearful husband will have an occasional lapse and display the feelings that dwell in his innermost heart, so Descartes, as he discusses a particular case, will proffer a remark that is at odds with his official wisdom. And as we have seen, this is most apt to happen when feelings or emotions are what is being talked about, as in the comment that "those who are most agitated by their passions are not the ones who know them best."

Let me make a final remark about Descartes and consciousness, prompted by the line that I have just quoted. If, as he says, I am sometimes not the one who knows my feelings best, this must mean that someone else knows them better. This happens often enough. A stranger watching me forever drop names as I engage in conversation may diagnose that I have low self-esteem: he or she is now better acquainted with my psyche than I am – one might say that in this respect my state, so far from being private, is in fact the opposite. One might call it *counterprivate*. And of course counterprivacy is even more our fate when we make mistakes. When Malvolio foolishly believes that Olivia loves him, other members of the household can laugh at his delusion; but he himself cannot – if he did, he would not be deluded. So, a mistake involves at least two divides: one between the person who makes it, and reality; and another, between that person and the witnesses to the mistake. As we have seen, Descartes in the *Meditations* devoted much thought to the first of these discords – he accounted for it in the end by discerning in us a faculty of idealization, which he called the *will*. But he is also quite alive to the second. In the letter of November 1646, where he sings the praise of the passions, he tells Chanut that he has taken the following as his motto,

> A sad death awaits him
> Who, too well known to all,
> Dies unknown to himself,

and so decided not to write any more books.[3] Think once more of *Meditation Two*, and of Descartes looking out of his window at creatures whom he calls *men*, but who might be automata wearing hats and coats. The supposition, there, pointed to a ravine between himself and others: he was directly acquainted with his own mental states; but for everyone else, he had to infer what those states were, and even infer that they existed at all. Well, the 1646 motto also points to a ravine, but this time the other way around. Other people might know what Descartes' passions are, or his false beliefs, while he himself does not or perhaps even cannot. Again, he is at a distance from other humans – a fitting image, it seems, of Cartesianism.

And yet, in a book that he will publish (resolve notwithstanding!) three years after the letter to Chanut, that distance will in an important way be eroded. Let us look at that development; it will be our sole glimpse at Descartes' moral psychology.

The *Passions of the Soul* is not an engaging text; in fact, it is doubtful that it was much read in Descartes' time, or after. The format does not help. In line perhaps with the prefatory announcement that the book will study the passions scientifically – *en physicien* (= as a physicist would: AT 11, 326; CSM 1, 327) – the reader is treated to a succession of numbered paragraphs, 212 of them – quite a fractured path, if you compare it with the smooth ramp of the *Meditations*. Also, over and above its *physicien* aspect, the detail is quite complicated. The book has three parts, in the last two of which Descartes will list, define, describe, and discuss more than 40 passions. Not unnaturally, the reader gets caught in the particulars and has trouble discerning a general course. Perhaps there is no general course, beyond the one charted by the principle that the passions "are all by nature good, and we have nothing to avoid but their misuse or their excess" (art. 211: AT 11, 485–6; CSM 1, 403). This means, for example, that hatred, envy, cowardice, and mockery are inherently good; while impudence and thanklessness (which are inherently bad) are not feelings or passions at all, but blamable ways of behaving. In the coming pages I shall discuss very little of the work as a whole, but confine myself to one thread in its vast fabric, a thread that begins with the study of *wonder*.

First, a bit of background. "Passion" (*passion*, in French) is Descartes' single word for what we would today call by an array of names, such as "feeling" or "mood" or "emotion." Also, following earlier writers, Descartes holds that there are primitive passions; primitive, in the sense that all the other passions (call them "particular") are species or combinations of them. Cheerfulness, for instance, is a species of joy (art. 210); and derision, a compound of joy and hatred: it is joy at some ill-fate that deservedly befalls a disliked person (art. 178). There are indefinitely many particular passions (art. 68), while the primitive ones are few – six, to be exact:[4] wonder, love, hatred, desire, joy, and sadness (art. 69). Let us, then, fix our sights on the first in the list, "the first of all the passions" (art. 53).

In Descartes' French, the word is *admiration* – not very easy to translate, even into modern French. *Admiration*, as commonly understood, is what you might feel when you see the Pyramids of Egypt – one of the seven wonders of the world. In that sense, "wonder" is an apt English translation; "marvel" might be another. Here, however, is what Descartes writes:

> when the first encounter with some object surprises us and we judge it to be new, or vastly different from what we formerly knew or supposed it would be, this causes us to wonder [*nous admirons*] and be astonished at it. (Art. 53: AT 11, 373; CSM 1, 350)

According to this gloss, you would not feel wonder the second time you looked at the Pyramids; or you would feel it only at the sight of a detail that you had previously missed. The definition also makes it possible for *admiration* to be negative – to include, for instance, my reaction to being served a tasteless meal in a swanky restaurant. If we stick to article 53, then "awe" seems the better rendering, since it makes ampler room for the bipolarity of the feeling – room for both the *plus* and the *minus*: many of my students would affix the word "awesome" to the Pyramids, and I will happily declare that my meal in the restaurant was awful. As it happens, today's colloquial French has a word that carries exactly the bipolar sense that so struck Descartes: it is the adjective *terrible* – affixable both to the Pyramids and to the meal!

Let me nonetheless retain "wonder" or "marvel" as my standard translation; and let us also keep in mind the emphasis on surprise that it involves, and on which Descartes insists. We are told for example (art. 72) that "surprise is special to this passion"; and soon afterward (art. 75), that "we wonder only at what appears to us rare and extraordinary." So be it. In fact, we are about to encounter a special rarity.

Humans have occasion to marvel at many things in their lives, but one target, Descartes thinks, is especially inviting – their own self; and not just anything in that self, but one particular feature:

> 151. [This] passion is remarkable when we refer it to ourselves, i.e. when it is our own merit for which we have esteem or contempt.
> 152. . . . I see only one thing in us which could give us good reason to esteem ourselves, namely the use of our free will and the dominion we have over our volitions. For we can reasonably be praised or blamed only for actions that depend on this free will; and it renders us in a certain way

like God, by making us masters of ourselves – provided we do not through cowardice lose the rights that it gives us.

These lines are near the beginning of Part 3 (AT 11, 444–5; CSM 1, 383–4). I have quoted at some length, both for what the text says and for what it will lead up to.

We might note that the two articles speak not of *marveling*, but of our *esteeming* ourselves. This is not a greatly significant difference, for esteem (according to the article that precedes the ones I have just quoted) is a species of wonder, its temporal extension as it were. Imagine the following scenario. One day, the thought that I had free will struck me, and filled me with wonder at myself: I was like God! That sentiment has now survived, perhaps not in its vivid initial form, but in the allied feeling of self-esteem: and it will go on surviving unless I lose it through cowardice – see the final warning of art. 152. Obviously there is a lot to ponder here. What exactly is the vision of free will that makes me esteem myself so highly? What kind of self-esteem does this foster? Why does cowardice threaten it? Cowardice at what? As I have said before, the fragmented and terse style of the *Passions* will often force one to make guesses about what lies behind the words; I hope to keep my guessing to a minimum, by also peering at other texts.

First, then, free will (*libre arbitre*). It is mentioned a number of times in the opening pages of Part 3 – even called "marvelous" at one point (art. 160); but we are never told what it amounts to, or why we should marvel. For further understanding, it will help to turn to the book that Descartes wrote a few years before, namely the *Principles*; for there, will and freedom are discussed at some length (arts. 37–43 of Part 1: AT 8a, 18–21; CSM 1, 205–7). Please observe that I am not turning back to *Meditation Four*.

The *Principles* do not mention marveling; but their account of free will does begin with the statement that "*the supreme perfection of man is that he acts freely or voluntarily*" – that is the title of article 37. The article then explains why freedom is such a supreme perfection: its presence means that we are not machines or automata, we are "in a special way the authors of our actions." In other words (art. 41), our free acts are undetermined (*indeterminatæ*). Now you might ask, how does Descartes – how do we? – know that they are? Answer (title of article 39): *the freedom of the will is self-evident*; and two articles later: "we have such close awareness of the freedom and indifference which is in us, that there is nothing we can grasp more evidently or more perfectly" (AT 8a, 20; CSM 1, 206). Note the word *indifference*: as we have seen, it is a term of art, designating the power to do-or-not-do. When I exert that power, my act proceeds from me, not necessitated or determined by any previous factor. Free will, in this sense, is a power of absolute origination: to repeat, we are "in a special way the authors of our actions." And although Descartes does not make the comparison in the *Principles*, one can see how the thought of this freedom might lead to the mental episode described in the *Passions* – our likening ourselves to God. God is indifferent, too.[5]

Add two twists to the plot. The first is a further contrast between human beings and machines. We, humans, can be praised for how we behave; machines cannot: "it is the designer who is praised for constructing such carefully-made devices; for in constructing them he acted not out of necessity but freely" (art. 37). Descartes must be restricting praise to a special kind, *moral* praise – after all, we can laud a clock for its accuracy. But given the restriction, we now meet an ancient puzzle. Yes, we do praise humans in their capacity of moral agents; but how to justify the praise, if it requires that their free acts be undetermined? After all, we too have a designer: God. Everything that happens in the world, including our so-called free acts, was preordained by that designer – Descartes states this quite categorically in article 40: it is "impious [*nefas*] to suppose that we could ever do anything that was not already preordained by him." Which leads at once to the question: how can the same act be both preordained and undetermined? Descartes' answer is simple: it *can* be both, and we are not to try to understand how:

> [W]e cannot get a sufficient grasp of [God's power] to see how it leaves the free actions of men undetermined. Still . . . it would be absurd, simply because we do not grasp one thing which we know must by its very nature be ungraspable, to doubt something else of which we have an intimate grasp and which we experience in ourselves. (Art. 41: AT 8a, 20; CSM 1, 206)

Once more we must compose with God's immensity – perhaps a further ground for marveling.

So much for the *Principles*; let us return to the *Passions* and to the feeling of self-esteem that the proper recognition of our free will is said to foster in us. Descartes has a name for that feeling: he calls it "generosity" (art. 153) – a species of esteem, then; *ergo* a species of wonder. Generosity can play a prominent role in our lives, a role that Descartes charts in that third and final part of the *Passions*; my final pages will be about it.

Once again we are meeting a word used in a broader sense than is common. As Descartes points out in article 161, it is meant to designate the feeling or virtue that moralists have traditionally called *magnanimity* – involving not just thoughts and attitudes toward other human beings, but also, and perhaps even more basically, thoughts and attitudes toward ourselves. Don't forget, generosity is a kind of self-esteem. Descartes will, over twelve or so articles of Part 3, draw a portrait of the generous person; but he does it in general terms and at times quite laconically: so it may help to consider an example, albeit a semi-imaginary one.

My name is Louis de Bretteville, and I am a pupil in the third grade at La Flèche (look back to the appendix of chapter 4). Sad to say, I am a *D*-student (where *D* means *dubious*), so made to sit in the last row of the class. But I am well-born; and since "there is no virtue as influenced by good birth as the one that causes us to esteem ourselves at our true value" (art. 161), I do esteem myself at my true value – that value being that I have a free will. So I am generous. How does this show? How does it affect my thoughts or actions? Well, to begin with, it means that I feel no envy or jealousy whatever of the classmates who sit ahead of me; I feel none, because I do not think myself inferior to them (art. 154). I bask in the feeling that I, no less than they, am a creature of free will and can, no less than they, use that will to good effect. In this sense I regard myself as their equal, just as entitled to be the friend of, say, Jean de la Porte (look again at the appendix to chapter 4) as his fellow front-row peers are. Even though I sit far back, I hold my head high; my shoulders are not hunched; I do not seek to ingratiate myself with anyone. I do not kowtow. Also, I regard myself just as entitled as the front-row-sitters are to raise my hand and ask a question, and I expect Father Vatier, our teacher, to pay just as much attention to it as he does to theirs. If, however, he does not, I feel no anger or resentment, for such feelings are beneath me. So it is that "generosity serves as a remedy against all the disorders of the passions" – title of article 156. And of course, what holds of me also holds of Jean de la Porte, if he is generous: he will not feel superior to anyone, at least not much.

> Just as [generous people] do not think themselves much inferior to those who have more wealth or honors, nor even to those who have more intelligence or knowledge or beauty, or, generally, to those who surpass them in some other perfection, so they do not esteem themselves much above those whom they surpass. For all these things seem to them of little significance in comparison with the good will for which alone they esteem themselves, and which they also suppose to be – or be at least capable of being – in every other person. (Art. 154: AT 11, 446–7; CSM 1, 384)

In this manner, generosity is not just a deterrent to ill feelings, but also a supreme equalizer: no matter where I sit, generosity makes me the peer of every student in the class.

Descartes may stand outside tradition in putting so much emphasis on etiology and feelings – remember, he ascribes the birth of generosity to a personal experience of awe: "I am a free being, like God!" But as far as the virtue itself goes, he appears to say little that moralists since

Aristotle have not already stressed:[6] after all, magnanimity has for millennia been a much lauded virtue. So the Cartesian eulogy looks prosaic enough – at least at first sight. As one looks more closely, however, it is difficult to escape the feeling that somehow there is more to the story than has emerged so far. It is not that one meets further chapters; rather, the odd cryptic remark makes one pause and reflect. Let me fasten on one or two of these curios.

Take the opening words of article 152 that I quoted a few pages ago (p. 126): "I see only one thing in us which could give us good reason to esteem ourselves, namely the use of our free will." Does this mean, then, that writing intelligent essays gives Jean de la Porte no reason to esteem himself? Isn't Descartes being a little narrow-minded? Nor is this a chance remark: he will repeat it not once but twice. Article 157: "all who conceive a good opinion of themselves for any other reason, whatever it may be, do not possess true generosity, but only vanity [orgueil] – which is always a vice." Article 158: "any other cause of self-esteem, whatever it may be, produces a highly blameworthy vanity." So: Jean de la Porte may feel happy about writing good essays, but he is not on that account allowed to "conceive a good opinion" of himself. Satisfaction, yes; self-esteem, no.

There is perhaps an escape. One might argue that the fine essays *do* entitle their author to self-esteem – but in a roundabout way: he may view them as achievements made possible through his free will. After all, each word, each sentence, came from him alone; it was up to him to pen it or not. The same holds true, for example, of the climber who has just scaled the North Face of the Eiger. Thinking well of oneself on account of what one has achieved thanks to one's will is very different from reveling in one's good looks or some other gift of nature. *Those* are displays of vanity; whereas, by contrast, student and climber have in no way ceased to be generous. Granted, this line of defense rather stretches the notion of generosity; but perhaps it bears stretching.

However, we may also wish to head in a different direction – prompted by another quirk in the text. Look at the same article 152, this time its final line: the declaration that free will makes us like God, "provided we do not lose through cowardice [lâcheté] the rights [droits] that it gives us." Here are surely words to marvel at – marvel, in the Cartesian sense. That rights should be invoked is no surprise: Descartes' century is when they come onto the scene. But in this instance we want to know more: what rights does our free will give us? How does cowardice deprive us of them? What cowardice? Descartes stays silent – nowhere in the book does he explicitly return to the subject. Given his muteness, we can only speculate; and it may help to go back to our La Flèche classroom, this time to a another D-student, call him Joseph Saillanfest, also sitting in the back row.

Just as his classmates are, Saillanfest is entitled to raise his hand and ask questions; and he is entitled to have them taken seriously. These rights accrue to him from the mere fact that he is a student, a human being, not an automaton; he is owed respect. But he may also lose these rights, for example if his questions are always insolent or inane: Father Vatier may simply ignore his raised hand. Few rights are inalienable; most of them can be lost through misdeed or misdemeanor. So far, so plain. But stretching the word a little, we might also speak of *loss* in a different sort of situation. Imagine that Saillanfest keeps mum because of the derisive laugh that his past questions have aroused from the rest of the class. He has now renounced his right to speak, from fear of mockery; and not just renounced: we might say that he has *lost* it – lost it through cowardice. And we might stretch that last word to cover an even more radical kind of forfeiture. Imagine that, because of his poor standing, Saillanfest does not even see himself as having the right to speak in the first place: he sits low in his chair, does not hold his head high, grovels to the teacher and to classmates. His condition is one of *abjectness* or *servility*, close cousins of cowardice; and his loss is now constitutional, caused by a certain vision of himself: he has lost self-respect.

So let us return to that final line of article 152 and its enigmatic mention of rights. On the reading that I propose and have sought to illustrate via tales of La Flèche students, Descartes is voicing this thought: we are, like God, masters of ourselves – provided we do not, through being servile, lose the self-respect that our free will enables us to have. The proviso, then, is about servility and self-respect. Of course one wants to ask, how much of this is actually in the text? Well, Descartes certainly talks about servility: he calls it *bassesse* or *humilité vicieuse,* and devotes article 159 (AT 11, 450; CSM 1, 386) to its description. The characteristic semi-physical, semi-mental postures are there: base spirits, we are told, "feel weak," they "shamefully abase themselves before those from whom they expect some advantage." More important, *bassesse* is said to be "directly opposed" to generosity – an opposition that might well be expressed, even in the seventeenth century, in terms of thinking-oneself versus not-thinking-oneself the bearer of certain rights. The generous person thinks himself such a bearer; the servile person does not.

On the other hand, Descartes never speaks of *self-respect*; and we should take that silence seriously, for it points to an important divide. We can focus on it by looking at the description he gives in article 164 of respect itself (AT 11, 455–6; CSM 1, 388–9). After pointing out that we can bestow it rightly or wrongly, he continues:

> the more noble and generous our soul is, the more inclined we are to render everyone his own; . . . we have no aversion to rendering all the honor and

respect that is due to men – to each according to the rank and authority he has in the world . . .

Please notice what is here called a person's "own" (*ce qui lui appartient*): it is the respect and honor that go with the rank (*rang*) and authority (*autorité*) that the person has. Rank and authority are of course on a scale; Father Vatier has more than the school janitor. So, respect is on a scale too: students will have more for the father than for the janitor. Nor is there anything remarkable in this way of speaking – respect, so understood, is a traditionally recognized attitude.

However, so understood (and let me call this the *scalar* sense), respect is no constitutive element of "true generosity"; in fact, the two are even in some way at odds, as Descartes himself intimates – why else assert that the generous person has no aversion (*répugnance*) to rendering respect? Where is the tension? Look again at article 154, and the distribution of esteem that it describes:

> Just as [generous people] do not think themselves much inferior to those who have more wealth or honors, nor even to those who have more intelligence or knowledge or beauty, or, generally, to those who surpass them in some other perfection, so they do not esteem themselves much above those whom they surpass. (AT 11, 446–7; CSM 1, 384)

So Louis de Bretteville may *respect* Father Vatier vastly more than the janitor; but he will *esteem* them equally, since on the score of esteem he views himself as the equal of both – not below the father, not above the janitor (disregard the adverb in the quotation). The esteem that goes with generosity, then, is egalitarian, non-scalar, absolute. Today, we often use the word "respect" to denote that attitude; we speak of respecting the janitor "as a person" – of respecting his autonomy, his rights. We also speak of respecting ourselves. Descartes, on the other hand, operates with two words (two worlds?): the older one, connected with rank and honor; and the other, which he is ready to link, however fleetingly, to the possession of rights. He does not, of course, speak of autonomy or of persons (in our heavy sense) – that vocabulary has yet to be born. His word is *generosity*.

We can now understand why Descartes should condemn all self-esteem not based on the thought of free will – remember article 157: "all who conceive a good opinion of themselves for any other reason, whatever it may be, do not possess true generosity, but only vanity." The odium turns on what he takes "conceiving a good opinion" to mean – when the opinion is about a person. Jean de la Porte, our *A*-student, is quite entitled to believe that he deserves more academic *respect* than the back-row-sitters: his work is better, his rank is higher, he sits in the front row. But he is not on that account entitled to "conceive a good opinion" of himself, for this means that he will esteem the back-sitters less, take them to have less claim to the teacher's attention, less right to ask questions; in short, regard them as lesser folk. *That* attitude is vanity. So, Descartes' disapproval turns on the narrow meaning he gives to the verbs *esteem* and *conceive a good opinion of* when their object is people (including oneself). We are entitled to a good opinion of ourselves only on grounds which will not distance us from others, grounds which we all share – that we are creatures of free will.

Some final thoughts. Descartes' correspondents, writing in Latin or French, would have a harder time formulating the question that follows, but in English it is simple: how often have we, at important junctures in Descartes' path, met the suffix "self" or "selves"? If you reflect, it is not a short count.

Look back to *Meditation Two*. It begins with the *cogito*, and this brings Descartes at once (AT 7, 25; CSM 2, 17) to ask about *ego ille*, "this I," that he now knows to exist: what is its nature? He discovers that it is *idem ego*, "the same I," that thinks, imagines and has sensations; and none of these activities can be separated from *ego ipse*, from "myself" (AT 7, 29; CSM 2, 19). He also discovers that no matter how well acquainted he is with the wax that he is now contemplating, he knows *ego ipse* better (AT 7, 33; CSM 2, 22), because thought always comes with the thought of himself. This is *Meditation Two*.

If anything, *ego ipse* plays an even more central role in the next leg. Descartes reflects that he will not know that there is anything in the world beside (him)self, unless he finds in his mind an idea that he (him)self could not have originated (AT 7, 42; CSM 2, 29). Providentially, he does find one idea that could not have come from (him) alone (*ego solus*) – the idea of God (AT 7, 45; CSM 2, 31). So God exists.

Next, *Meditation Four*. As we saw, its tone is quasi-forensic: has he, Descartes, not the right to complain of having been created so defective, so apt to make countless mistakes? The verdict is *no*. It is he himself who is ultimately responsible, not God: for he was created such that he could withhold assent whenever an idea of his was not clear and distinct enough, and so avoid making a mistake. Descartes has only himself to blame.

Ego ipse is also a prominent sight at the highest coil in Descartes' progress, the proof of mind–body distinction in *Meditation Six*. He finds that he can have a clear idea of (him)self without thinking of any bodily object; and vice versa. So he (that is, his mind) and his body are really distinct. As one looks back, it seems entirely fitting that the thought of Descartes' *ego ipse* should culminate in a proof of *distinction*: has that thought not always come onto the scene so as to separate one thing from another? – whether it be, as in *Meditation Four*, to set Descartes' responsibility apart from God's; or, as in *Meditation Three*, to set his idea of God apart from all his other ideas; or, as in *Meditation Two*, to distinguish his acquaintance with his own mind from his acquaintance with anything else in the world, be it wax or persons?

Given this harsh fact, it is all the more remarkable that when it appears in Descartes' final work – in the fragment of the *Passions* that we have just considered – the idea of ourselves should come not as a divider, but, on the contrary, as a strong unifier. Granted, the story begins in Descartes' usual manner: the self-attention that gives birth to generosity turns on a contrast – unlike machines, we have free will, we can be praised or blamed. But the feeling that emerges from this attention has a wonderful unifying power, it prevents us from seeing ourselves as superior or inferior to other humans. More engagingly still,

> those who have this feeling about themselves . . . never have contempt for anyone. Although they often see that others do wrong in ways that show their weakness, they are nevertheless more inclined to excuse than to blame them and to regard such wrongdoing as due rather to lack of knowledge than to lack of good will. (Art. 154: AT 11, 446; CSM 1, 384)

So, we shall excuse rather than blame, perhaps even deceiving ourselves in the process.

When Hegel called Descartes the true founder of modern philosophy, odds are that he did not have in mind the *Passions of the Soul*, or even the last few pages of the last *Meditation*. Yet the thoughts we find there are hardly trivial. That the body of the dropsical man is not like an ill-functioning clock, that the very idiom of malady presupposes a stronger link between mind and body than mere interaction: these are provocative ideas, surely. So is the doctrine that we contemplated in the last few pages – that seeing people as bearers of rights, respecting them as persons, has its origins not in the intellect but in our emotions, in a feeling of wonder that we have about ourselves, wonder at being creatures of free will. Rich though these thoughts may be, they do not belong to the vision of Descartes that posterity has preserved.

One might reply: the reason for the neglect is that they are really afterthoughts, not voiced with the integrity that graces official Cartesianism. To give substance to the remarks about dropsy and mind–body intermixture, scholars need to invoke passages in other works, or in the correspondence. And since these props are unavailable for the *Passions*, readers will resort to an even more devious strategy – they will (as I myself have done) look at the words through lenses colored by knowledge of what happened afterward. So while there may be grounds for interest in Descartes' later work, there are perfectly good reasons for regarding that work as no more than an interesting side-show, not the main act.

True enough. But there are probably more intense reasons why we think there *is* a main act, and why it is so short – basically *Meditations One* and *Two*; add, if you wish, the paragraph in *Meditation Six* about real distinction, plus perhaps Part 4 and (end of) Part 5 of the *Discourse*. These brief pages voice thoughts that are disturbing, and disturbing not merely to philosophers. They tell me, for example, that it is just my intellect which makes me what I am; that my body is distinct from me, in fact not all that different from my watch; that I am a world away from you, I can even suppose you to be a machine clad in human clothes; after all, your dog is no more than a machine. Many believe that these conclusions are false, but are more than a little drawn to them. Images of them populate science-fiction movies; and wonderfully, here is a philosopher who has argued for them. Do I want his words bleached by yet more words from his pen? Or do I prefer them stark and simple, so that I can be attracted and – disagree?

notes

preface

1 In the *letter* to her of May 18, 1645: AT 4, 201; not in CSMK. See chapter 1 for an explanation of these references.
2 Nicolas Fontaine: *Mémoires pour servir à l'histoire de Port-Royal*, 1736, vol. II, pp. 52–4; in Frédéric Delforge: *Les petites écoles de Port-Royal* (Paris, 1985), p. 97.
3 In *The Treasury of the Encyclopedia Britannica*, ed. Clifton Fadiman (New York: Viking, 1992), p. 72. In a *letter* to Morus, February 5, 1649 (AT 5, 279; CSMK, 366), Descartes does say that his view "absolves human beings from the suspicion of crime when they eat or kill animals."
4 Cf. *letter* to Newcastle, October 23, 1646: AT 4, 574; CSMK, 303. Nor can this be a slip: Descartes is explaining to the Marquess his doctrine about animals.
5 *Reply* to *Fourth* set of *Objections*: AT 7, 246; CSM 2, 171.
6 *Passions of the Soul*, art. 28: AT 11, 349; CSM 1, 339.

chapter 1   life and writings

1 I owe this classification to Jean-Robert Armogathe, who is about to bring out a new edition of the correspondence.
2 Here, then, are references for some of the texts quoted in this chapter:
   (i)   about tears and women: *letter* to Pollot, mid-January 1641 (AT 3, 278; CSMK, 167);
   (ii) about hearing Calvinist preacher: *letter* to Mersenne, November 13, 1639 (AT 2, 620; not in CSMK);
   (iii) about personal motto: *letter* to Chanut, November 1, 1646 (AT 4, 537; CSMK, 300); also written as an autograph to Cornelis de Glarges, November 10, 1644 (AT 4, 726);
   (iv) about peripatetic philosophy: *Letter* to Dinet (AT 7, 580; CSM 2, 391).

chapter 2   distrust and deception

1 Here are some recent books on Descartes' scientific thought: William R. Shea, *The Magic of Numbers and Motion: The Scientific Career of René*

Descartes (Canton, MA: Science History Publications, 1991); Daniel Garber: *Descartes' Metaphysical Physics* (Chicago: University of Chicago Press, 1992); Stephen Gaukroger: *Descartes: An Intellectual Biography* (Oxford: Clarendon Press, 1995).

2 When was he tagged with the title? Philosophic lore doesn't say. In his *Lectures on the History of Philosophy*, Hegel calls Descartes the "true founder" (*wahrhaste Anfänger*) of modern philosophy (*Sämtliche Werke*, vol. 19, p. 331; for some reason, the words don't appear in the standard English translation). That appraisal has endured – a probable legacy, then, of post-Kantianism.

3 I exaggerate: this is true only of the first three *Meditations*. There is one break in *Meditation Four*; four in the next; and about a dozen in the last. Modern editions have not followed Descartes, they fracture the text throughout; one exception is Michelle Beyssade's recent edition of the *Méditations métaphysiques*.

4 Again I exaggerate, but only microscopically: Archimedes is mentioned in the *Second Meditation* (AT 7, 24; CSM 2, 16) as part of a figure of style.

5 These two contrasts don't always coincide. I have a friend who somehow seldom honors the commitments he makes, even to me; and so I have learnt not to rely on what he says. It's not that the pledges are insincere: at the time of pledging he intends to live up to them. I say that my friend is unreliable – he has that quirk in his make-up – in much the same way I would say that my old car is unreliable: in both cases, it is wise not to set one's expectations too high. We can distrust people without believing them to be deceitful or dishonest.

6 For recent dissents from this view, see Ian Hacking's "Dreams in place," in his *Historical Ontology* (Cambridge, MA: Harvard University Press, 2002); or Georges Moyal in his *Critique cartésienne de la raison* (Paris: Vrin, 1997).

7 John Donne: *Ten Sermons*, ed. Geoffrey Keynes (London: The Nonesuch Press, 1923), p. 92.

8 Francisco Suárez: *Disputationes theologicæ*, 12; and "De integritate confessionis" 10, in the *Tractatus de fide*, 1.3.5.

9 Hugo Grotius: "Deo, tanquam jus summum in homines habenti, . . . non conveni[t] mendacium." *De jure belli ac pacis*, 3.1.15.

10 For example, in the 1643 (?) *letter* to Buitendijck, a curator of the University of Utrecht (AT 4, 64; CSMK, 230); see also the May 4, 1647 *letter* to the curators of Leiden University (AT 5, 9; CSMK, 316).

11 For details, see Caroline Thijssen-Schoute, *Nederlands cartesianisme* (Amsterdam, 1954), pp. 48–9.

12 Hume: *An Enquiry Concerning Human Understanding*, section 12.

13 Though not part of the *Meditations*, this is an important text: it's in the *Reply* to the *Second* set of *Objections* (AT 7, 145–6; CSM 2, 104) – a passage where Descartes explicitly addresses Hume-type queries about the tenability and resolvability of the doubt.

14 This is not to deny that there are passages where Descartes plays down the uncomfortable character of the doubt. Every day is another day.

15 They are two paragraphs at the beginning of chapter 2 of *Histoire de la folie* (pp. 56–7, in the second edition) – paragraphs omitted from the English translation of the book, which came out in 1965 under the title *Madness and Civilization*.

16 In French, in *L'Écriture et la différence* (Paris: Seuil, 1967); in English, in Jacques Derrida, *Writing and Difference*, "Cogito and the History of Madness," pp. 31–63 (London: Routledge, 2001).

17 In French, this reply appeared as an addendum to the second edition of *Histoire de la folie* (1972), pp. 583–603. In English, it is to be found in Michel Foucault, *Essential Works*, vol. 2 (New York: The New Press, 1998), "My body, this paper, this fire," pp. 393–417.

18 Perhaps to challenge custom, CSM render the Latin as "malicious demon." I have restored the standard translation.

19 *Seventh* set of *Objections* (AT 7, 455 and 529; CSM 2, 305 and 360).

20 *Othello* was first performed in 1604, and published in 1622; Don Juan first stood on the stage in 1630, in Tirso de Molina's *El burlador de Sevilla y el convidado de piedra*.

21 Whether Darwinism makes it in fact easier to resist the "blind-force" argument is a debated matter. See for example Alvin Plantinga's *Warrant and Proper Function* (Oxford: Oxford University Press, 1993), esp. ch. 12.

chapter 3 me and others

1 For some unexplained reason, CSM translate the canonical sentence as "I am thinking, therefore I exist." I substitute the standard translation throughout.

2 The first to ask the question seems to have been the author of the *Second* set of *Objections* (AT 7, 125; CSM 2, 89); Descartes replied at AT 7, 140–1; CSM 2, 100. He was asked again, by Burman, in the *Conversation*; and we have his reply (AT 5, 147; CSMK, 333). See also his *letter* to Silhon (?), March or April 1648 (AT 5, 137–8; CSMK, 331). The secondary literature is of course immense: in fact, an entire book was published on this topic not long ago – Jerrold J. Katz, *Cogitations* (Oxford: Oxford University Press, 1986).

3 "*I think therefore I am* is the first and most certain of all propositions to occur to anyone who philosophizes in an orderly way": *Principles*, Part 1, art. 10 (AT 8a, 8; CSM 1, 196). Descartes in fact does not elucidate why the dictum is more certain than, say, *the whole is greater than the part*.

4 Remember the Norwegian letter that I quote at the beginning of this book: "Unlike Descartes I do not need to think in order to be."

5 Sometimes it is the second verb that is altered. Apparently in 1989, some Tiananmen Square demonstrators were wearing T-shirts with the motto "I think therefore I am dangerous." Marleen Rozemond tells me that in recent demonstrations in Holland against proposed budget cuts among teachers, there were posters saying "I think, therefore I am unemployed."

6 An interesting recent work on the importance of the doubt is Janet Broughton's *Descartes's Method of Doubt* (Princeton: Princeton University Press, 2002).

7 The last eight words are in the French version of the *Meditations* (AT 9a, 21) – more explicit here than the Latin (AT 7, 26–27). CSM's translation (2, 18) also seems to be a mixture of both. Incidentally, this passage features the final mention of the evil genius – from now on, the deceiving God will be alone on the stage.

8 A similar gloss of what it means to be a "thinking thing" occurs a few pages later, in the opening paragraph of the *Third Meditation*. In the French version of that paragraph (AT 9a, 27), love and hate are added to the list of "thoughts" – I owe this observation to Lilli Alanen.

9 "Nature or essence" is a phrase that occurs a number of times in Descartes, especially in French texts – for example Part 4 of the *Discourse* (AT 6, 33; CSM 1, 127), or the French version of *Meditation Six* (AT 9a, 58); for "*natura seu essentia,*" see the *Notæ* (AT 8b, 355; CSM 1, 302).

10 Respectively: *Third* set of *Objections* (AT 7, 178; CSM 2, 125–6; Descartes' *Reply* follows immediately); and *Fifth* set (AT 7, 271–5; CSM 2, 189–191; Descartes' *Reply* is at AT 7, 359; CSM 2, 248).

11 Interestingly, in article 138 of the *Passions* (AT 11, 431; CSM 1, 377) Descartes speaks of animals being "deceived" (*trompés*) by lures – doubtless a lapse into common ways of talking. His most extended account of the role of judgment in perception is in the *Sixth Replies* (AT 7, 437–8; CSM 2, 294–5).

12 See note 2 of the Preface.

13 Remembering Freud (*Civilization and its Discontents*, 1; SE 21, 64–73), one might also call it *oceanic*.

14 The phrase will occur twice more in the *Meditations*, at AT 7, 28 and AT 7, 49; a synonym, *is ego* (*eo me*, in the ablative), is at AT 7, 27; CSM 2, 18 – our text [D]. Descartes also speaks of the "same 'I' " (*ego idem*) at AT 7, 29; CSM 2, 19. In French, he says "ce moi," for example in a *letter* to Colvius, November 14, 1640 (AT 3, 247; CSMK, 159).

15 A similar unease must have affected the English translators confronting Freud's "*das Ich.*" They opted for Latinization, with the result that "ego" is now a quasi-current English noun.

chapter 4   me and my maker

1 Descartes discusses the idea of the elaborate machine at greater length in his *Reply* to the *First* set of *Objections*, AT 7, 103–5; CSM 2, 75–6).

2 The axiom appears *verbatim* neither in the *Principles* nor in *Meditation Three*. But as we have seen, Descartes invoked a close cousin in *Meditation One* – against the atheist who claimed immunity from the doubt on the ground that he did not believe in any God, let alone one who deceived. Descartes replied that the atheist had, if anything, greater reason to doubt: since he must believe that he has come about not through God's design, but by a succession of natural causes, and since "*the less accomplished the maker, the less accomplished the product,*" the atheist must hold that he is very imperfect – hence apt to be always mistaken.

3 74a–76c.

4 *Ratio studiorum* (Paris: Belin, 1997), ch. 16, "Common rules for teachers of younger classes"; sect. 38, "Class-list" (= 16–38); p. 162.

5 In French and Dutch, the word is "*carrière*"; in German, "Karriere"; in Spanish, "carriera." All these words, the dictionaries tell us, are descended from the late Latin *via carraria* – "race course for horse-carriages." Indeed, at first the term will simply mean "course," as, for instance, the *career of the*

sun; but it will soon evolve and come to designate the course of human life insofar as it affords opportunities for advancement (or non-advancement).

6 Joseph de Jouvancy, *De ratione discendi et docendi* (Paris: Dabo-Butshert, 1701), p. 161.

7 Descartes had already voiced the contrast between grasping (= "embracing") and discerning (= "touching with one's mind") ten years earlier, in a *letter* to Mersenne, May 27, 1630 (AT 1, 152; CSMK, 25); and he will repeat it in 1647, in the *letter* to Clerselier appended to the French version of the *Fifth* set of *Replies* (AT 9a, 210; CSM 2, 273–4).

8 Actually, there is already a whiff of proof at the end of *Meditation Three* (AT 7, 52; CSM 2, 35).

9 For a summary of some recent discussions, see Louis Loeb, "The Cartesian Circle" in the *Cambridge Companion to Descartes*, ed. J. Cottingham (Cambridge: Cambridge University Press, 1992).

10 This is in the *Elements*, IX, 20. Suppose the list of primes to be finite, say <2, 3, 5, . . . , N>, where N is the largest prime. Take the product <2 × 3 × 5 . . . × N>; add 1; and call that number "S." Either S is a prime or it is not. If it is, then it is obviously greater than N. And if S is not prime, then it is not divisible without remainder by any member of <2, 3, 5 . . . , N> – there will always be the remainder 1. So again, there is a prime greater than N. So the list is not finite.

11 The equation of certainty with *illumination* or *light* is frequent in the seventeenth century, and in Descartes – he defends the image against Hobbes's *Objection* (AT 7, 191–2; CSM 2, 134–5). For this topic in general, see Nicholas Jolley: *The Light of the Soul* (Oxford: Clarendon Press, 1990).

12 These lines are at the end of *Meditation Five*, where Descartes returns to the topic of God and certainty. The same view is stated, even more emphatically, in a *letter* to Regius, May 24, 1640 (AT 3, 64–5; CSMK, 147).

chapter 5   deception and rights

1 There is an almost parallel text in *Principles* 1, 29 (AT 8a, 16; CSM 1, 203).

2 See chapter 2 of this book, pp. 19–20.

3 As it happens, most of these words crossed over in the century around the *Meditations*.

4 Don Juan saw literary light of day in Tirso de Molina's *El burlador de Sevilla* (*The Trickster of Seville*), around 1630.

5 For example Paracelsus – this would be in the mid-1500s – warns liars against "destroying their own heart" (*Selected Writings*, p. 166): destroying one's heart, corrupting one's soul – these are obviously kindred thoughts.

6 "3.1.11" means: book 3, chapter 1, section 11. Descartes never mentions Grotius, let alone the *De jure*. Yet it is almost impossible that he should not have known the book. The *De jure* came out in 1625 in Paris, and was the subject of widespread discussion in the circles in which Descartes moved.

7 Here for instance is the article on *le mensonge* in vol. 10 of the *Encyclopédie* (1751–80):

Lying consists in deliberately expressing oneself, in words or signs, in a way that is false . . . when he to whom we speak has a right to know our thoughts. . . . We do not lie each time that we speak in a manner that does not correspond to our thoughts. . . . It is therefore a mistake not to distinguish between *lying* and *telling a falsehood.* Lying is a dishonest and blameworthy act; but we may utter a falsehood that is indifferent, or permitted, or praiseworthy, or even required. Such a falsehood must not be confused with a lie. . . . We should therefore not accuse of lying those who use a fiction for the purpose of instructing, or to protect an innocent, or to appease a madman who is about to hurt us; or to make the sick take their medication.

8 *Les Rêveries du promeneur solitaire,* p. 78. Just before this passage, Rousseau writes that he has spent a lifetime thinking about lies and lying.
9 *The Dictionary Historical and Critical of Mr. Peter Bayle* (1734–8), excerpted in R. Ariew and E. Watkins, eds., *Readings in Modern Philosophy,* vol. 2 (Indianapolis: Hackett, 2000), p. 235.
10 Descartes also alludes to it in *Meditation Six* (at AT 7, 77; CSM 2, 53).
11 This is from the *Second* set of *Replies* (AT 7, 143; CSM 2, 102) – words that come almost immediately after Descartes' reply to Mersenne (quoted on p. 73) about God not being a deceiver.
12 Kant explains the phrase at some length in the *Foundations of the Metaphysics of Morals* (ed. Lewis White Beck; Chicago: University of Chicago Press, 1949), p. 86. Incidentally, unlike French (or English), Latin for *duty* is no kin of *debere*: the standard word is *officium* – it does not appear in the body of the *Meditations.*
13 The example of the poisoned apple is actually offered by Descartes, to explain his doctrine of error (*Fifth* set of *Replies,* AT 7, 376–377; CSM 2, 259): I discuss it in the next chapter. 464731 can be divided by 3119 and by 149.

chapter 6 idealization

1 *Twilight of the Idols,* "The four great errors": sect. 3, "The error of false causality": "The 'inner world' is full of phantoms and will-o'-the-wisps: the will is one of them."
2 189d–193a.
3 *De natura rerum,* bk 4, 1149–66: as a matter of fact, Molière had in his youth worked on a translation of that poem. The passage of the *Misanthrope* is lines 717–30, Act II, sc. iv, translated by Richard Wilbur, in *Molière: Four Comedies* (London and New York: Harcourt Brace Jovanovich, 1982), pp. 216–17.
4 This is in *Group Psychology and the Analysis of the Ego,* ch. 8 (*Standard edition,* vol. 18, p. 112).
5 Incidentally, "*se joindre de volonté*" is an odd phrase – even in seventeenth-century French.
6 *A Midsummer Night's Dream,* Act III, sc. i: "Mine ear is much enamour'd of thy note."
7 This is from Spinoza's *Ethics* (Part III, proposition 9, Scholium).

8 In the February 1647 *letter* to Chanut, Descartes does speak a few times (at AT 4, 612; CSMK, 311) of love as the "joining oneself by will" to another person; but the word "assent" does not appear.

9 I have translated the last sentence quite freely. The Latin says: *possumus de eadem re velle permulta, et perpauca tantum cognoscere* – "about one and the same thing, we can will a great deal, and only know very little."

10 Whether there really is a gap is a matter of controversy too. Perhaps the first commentator to stress it was Ferdinand Alquié, in *La Découverte méta-physique de l'homme chez Descartes* (Paris, 1950), esp. ch. 14. On the opposite side stands, for example, Anthony Kenny, in "Descartes on the Will," in R. J. Butler (ed.), *Cartesian Studies* (New York: Barnes and Noble, 1972).

11 Dictionaries date the "bad" sense of the word to the late eighteenth century; "machination," on the other hand, has a longer past – the *OED* lists a fifteenth-century occurrence.

chapter 7   really distinct . . .

1 The key word was added to the title of the book in the 1647 French transla-tion – which Descartes is supposed to have overseen. Where the Latin had simply spoken of "the distinction between the human soul and the body" (*animæ humanæ a corpore distinctio*), the French said: "*la distinction réelle entre l'âme et le corps de l'homme*" (AT 9a, 13). In both Latin and French, "real distinction" also appears in the *Dedicatory letter to the Sorbonne* that comes before the *Meditations* proper (AT 7, 6; CSM 2, 6).

2 Descartes would call the distinction between "round" and "square" a *modal* one (*Principles*, 1–61: AT 8a, 29; CSM 1, 213–14).

3 This use is explained in article 1 of Part 2 of the *Principles* (AT 8a, 41; CSM 1, 223).

4 It was to be repeated, for example in 1644, in the *Principles*: "we have a clear understanding of [body] as something that is quite distinct from God and from ourselves or our mind" (same article as in the previous note). And it had been preceded by this post-*cogito* passage in the *Discourse* (AT 6, 33; CSM 1, 127): "this 'I' – that is the soul by which I am what I am – is entirely distinct from the body."

5 This was in public theses defended at Utrecht in December 1641. For more information on the Descartes–Regius nexus, see *La Querelle d'Utrecht*, ed. Theo Verbeek (Paris, 1988), esp. pp. 40–1.

6 Posterity has called the *petite glande* the "*pineal gland*": Descartes himself hardly ever uses the adjective – never in his published writings.

7 Descartes had used that image in the unpublished *Treatise on Man* (AT 11, 131; CSM 1, 101); and in the published work, as early as 1637, in Part 4 of the *Dioptrics* (AT 6, 129). It does not appear in the *Meditations*.

8 For example, in Daniel Garber's "Understanding interaction: what Des-cartes should have told Princess Elizabeth," in his *Descartes Embodied* (Cambridge: Cambridge University Press, 2001).

9 Descartes' references to children are almost always disparaging – a good example is articles 71 and 72 of part 1 of the *Principles*. The title of article 71 is: "The chief cause of error arises from the preconceived opinions of childhood," and its last sentence: "Right from our infancy our mind was swamped with a thousand of such preconceived opinions; and in later childhood, forgetting that they were adopted without sufficient examination, it regarded them as known by the senses or implanted by nature, and accepted them as utterly true and evident." Article 72 details how these preconceived opinions survive into adulthood.

10 Here is the *Conversation* with Burman (1648):

> Q: How can the soul be affected by the body and vice versa, when their natures are completely different?
> A: This is most difficult to explain; but here experience is sufficient, since experience is so clear here that it can in no way be denied. (AT 5, 163; CSMK, 346)

11 Apart from *Meditation Six* and the *Reply* to Arnauld, the main texts having to do with substantial union are the *Reply* to the *Sixth* set of *Objections* (AT 7, 423–4; CSM 2, 285–6); the *letter* to Father Dinet attached to the *Seventh* set of *Replies* (AT 7, 585); the *Principles*, Part 1, arts. 48 and 60; Part 2, art. 3; Part 4, art. 190; two *letters* to Regius, December 1641 (AT 3, 460–1; CSMK, 200) and January 1642 (AT 3, 492–3; CSMK, 206); and the May and June 1643 *letters* to the Princess.

12 Descartes wavered about angels. He wrote to Morus in August 1649 (AT 5, 402; CSMK 380): "it is not clear by mere natural reason whether angels are created like minds distinct from bodies, or like minds united to bodies. I never decide about questions about which I have no assured reasons." (Note the contrast drawn here between *distinct* and *united*; one might ask how it squares with *Meditation Six*.)

13 In fact, the literature about substantial union is considerable. Here are two recent books, in English, that discuss it in great detail: Marleen Rozemond, *Descartes's Dualism* (Cambridge, MA: Harvard University Press, 1998); and Lilli Alanen, *Descartes's Concept of Mind* (Cambridge, MA: Harvard University Press, 2003).

14 To Des Bosses, April 29, 1715 (Leibniz: *Philosophischen Schriften*, ed. C. I. Gerhardt, 2, 496; in English, in Leibniz, *Philosophical Papers and Letters*, ed. L. E. Loemker, 2nd edn. 611).

15 The doctrine is developed in the *Philosophical Investigations*. To my knowledge, Wittgenstein never actually names Descartes. The actual criticism was voiced mostly by one of his ex-students, O. K. Bouwsma, in a series of articles in the 1950s, later gathered in his *Philosophical Papers* (Liincoln: Unversity of Nebraska Press, 1965).

16 For Leibniz, individual beings – *monads* – are not created but come about by "fulguration" (*Monadology*, art. 3).

chapter 8   self-esteem

1 Antonio R. Damasio: *Descartes' Error* (New York: Putnam's, 1994).
2 The Freud quotation is from his *Introductory Lectures*, lecture 1 (SE 15, 21–2);
  see also *The Unconscious* (SE 14, 166–9). For Leibniz's advocacy of subliminal
  thinking, see, for instance, the Preface of the *New Essays*: "at every moment
  there is in us an infinity of perceptions unaccompanied by awareness [= *aper-
  ception*] or reflection" (Leibniz: *New Essays on Human Understanding*, ed.
  Peter Remnant and Jonathan Bennett (Cambridge: Cambridge University
  Press, 1981), p. 53). An interesting and informative study of the history of dissent from the mental-conscious equation is Henri Ellenberger's *Discovery of
  the Unconscious* (New York: Harper's, 1970).
3 AT 4, 537; CSMK, 300: I mentioned this motto in my brief biography of
  Descartes at the beginning of this book. It might be set beside one of the last
  entries in Wittgenstein's journal, a few days before his death: "God may say
  to me: I am judging you out of your own mouth. Your own actions have made
  you shudder with disgust when you have seen other people do them"
  (Wittgenstein, *Culture and Value* (Oxford: Blackwell, 1980), p. 87.
4 This is fewer than the standard scholastic list of 11, derived from Aquinas'
  Summa Theologica (Ia IIae, q.23, art. 4), to which Descartes refers disparag-
  ingly in article 68 – incidentally, that list did not include *wonder*. For information about seventeenth-century literature on the passions, see Anthony Levi,
  French Moralists: The Theory of the Passions, 1585–1649 (Oxford: Clarendon
  Press, 1964); and Susan James, *Passion and Action: The Emotions in
  Seventeenth-Century Philosophy* (Oxford: Clarendon Press, 1997).
5 "Although God is completely indifferent with respect to all things, he necessarily made the decrees he did": *Conversation with Burman* (AT 5, 166;
  CSMK, 348). Note the paradox.
6 The main Aristotelian text is the *Nicomachean Ethics*, book 4,
  1123a34–1125a35.

bibliography

Descartes, *Œuvres de Descartes*, ed. Charles Adam and Paul Tannery, 11 vols., rev. edn. (Paris: Vrin/CNRS, 1964–76).

Descartes, *The Philosophical Writings of Descartes*, trans. by John Cottingham, Robert Stoothoff, Dugald Murdoch, and Anthony Kenny, 3 vols. (Cambridge: Cambridge University Press, 1985–91).

Descartes, *Méditations métaphysiques*, éditées par Michelle Beyssade, Paris, Librairie générale française, 1990.

Descartes, *Œuvres complètes de René Descartes* (CD-ROM edition: Connaught Project-University of Toronto, Charlottesville, Intelex, 2001).

pre-twentieth century

Aquinas, *Summa Theologica* (many editions).

Aristotle, *Nicomachean Ethics* (many editions).

Augustine, *De mendacio*, in *St Augustin: Problèmes moraux* (Paris: Desclée de Brouwer, 1948).

Baillet, Adrien, *La Vie de M. Descartes*, 2 vols. (Paris, 1691).

Bayle, Pierre: *Dictionnaire historique et critique*, 4 vols. (Amsterdam: Reinier Leers, 1697).

Diderot, Denis, and Jean D'Alembert (eds.), *Encyclopédie*, 35 vols. (Paris, 1751–80).

Donne, John, *Ten Sermons*, ed. Geoffrey Keynes (London: The Nonesuch Press, 1923).

Euclid, *Elements of Geometry* (many editions).

Grotius, *De jure belli ac pacis*, ed. P. C. Molhuysen (The Hague: Sijthoff, 1919).

Hegel, Georg Wilhelm Friedrich, *Sämtliche Werke*, ed. H. Glockner, 26 vols. (Stuttgart: Frommann, 1965–8).

Hume, David, *An Enquiry Concerning Human Understanding*, in D. C. Yalden-Thomson (ed.), *Hume: Theory of Knowledge* (Edinburgh: Nelson, 1951).

Homer, *The Odyssey*, trans. Robert Fitzerald (New York: Doubleday, 1961).

Jouvancy, Joseph de, *De ratione discendi et docendi* (Paris: Dabo-Butshert, 1701).

Kant, Immanuel, *Foundations of the Metaphysics of Morals*, in Lewis White Beck (ed.), *Critique of Practical Reason and Other Writings in Moral Philosophy* (Chicago: University of Chicago Press, 1949).

Leibniz, Gottfried, *Philosophical Papers and Letters*, ed. Leroy E. Loemker, 2nd edn. (Dordrecht: Reidel, 1969).

Leibniz, Gottfried, *New Essays on Human Understanding*, ed. Peter Remnant and Jonathan Bennett (Cambridge: Cambridge University Press, 1981).

Molière, *Four Comedies*, trans. Richard Wilbur (London: Penguin, 1982).

Nietzsche, Friedrich, *Twilight of the Idols*, in Walter Kaufmann (ed.), *The Portable Nietzsche* (New York: Viking, 1954).

Paracelsus, *Selected Writings*, ed. Joland Jacobi (Princeton: Princeton University Press, 1951).

Plato, *Hippias Minor* (many editions).

Plato, *Phaedo* (many editions).

Plato, *Republic* (many editions).

Plato, *Symposium* (many editions).

Ratio studiorum (Paris: Belin, 1997).

Rochemonteix, Camille de, *Un Collège de jésuites aux XVIIe & XVIIIe siècles: le Collège Henri IV de La Flèche*, 4 vols. (Le Mans: Leguicheux, 1889).

Rousseau, Jean-Jacques, *Les Rêveries d'un promeneur solitaire* (Paris: Garnier, 1949).

Spinoza, Baruch, *Ethics*, ed. Edwin Curley (Princeton: Princeton University Press, 1988).

Suárez, Francisco, *Opera Omnia*, 26 vols. (Paris: Vivès, 1856–77).

contemporary

Alanen, Lilli, *Descartes's Concept of Mind* (Cambridge: Harvard University Press, 2003).

Alquié, Ferdinand, *La Découverte métaphysique de l'homme chez Descartes* (Paris: PUF, 1950).

Bouwsma, O. K., *Philosophical Papers* (Lincoln: University of Nebraska Press, 1965).

Broughton, Janet, *Descartes's Method of Doubt* (Princeton: Princeton University Press, 2002).

Butler, Ronald (ed.), *Cartesian Studies* (New York: Barnes and Noble, 1972).

Cottingham, John (ed.), *Cambridge Companion to Descartes* (Cambridge: Cambridge University Press, 1992).

Damasio, Antonio R., *Descartes' Error* (New York: Putnam's, 1994).

Delforges, Frédéric, *Les Petites Écoles de Port-Royal* (Paris, 1985).

Derrida, Jacques, *L'Écriture et la différence* (Seuil: Paris, 1967).

Ellenberger, Henri, *Discovery of the Unconscious* (New York: Harper's, 1970).

Foucault, Michel, *Histoire de la folie*, 2nd edn. (Paris: Gallimard, 1972).

Foucault, Michel, *Essential Works*, 2nd vol. (New York: The New Press, 1998).

Freud, Sigmund, *The Standard Edition of the Complete Psychological Works of Sigmund Freud*, ed. James Strachey, 24 vols. (London: Hogarth, 1953–74).

Garber, Daniel, *Descartes' Metaphysical Physics* (Chicago: University of Chicago Press, 1992).

Garber, Daniel, *Descartes Embodied* (Cambridge: Cambridge University Press, 2001).

Gaukroger, Stephen, *Descartes: An Intellectual Biography* (Oxford: Clarendon Press, 1995).

Hacking, Ian, *Historical Ontology* (Cambridge: Harvard University Press, 2002).

James, Susan, *Passion and Action: The Emotions in Seventeenth-Century Philosophy* (Oxford: Clarendon, 1997).

Jolley, Nicholas, *The Light of the Soul* (Oxford: Clarendon, 1990).

Katz, Jerrold, *Cogitations* (New York: Oxford University Press, 1986).

Levi, Anthony, *French Moralists: The Theory of the Passions, 1585–1649* (Oxford: Clarendon, 1964).

Moyal, Georges, *Critique cartésienne de la raison* (Paris: Vrin, 1997).

Plantinga, Alvin, *Warrant and Proper Function* (Oxford: Oxford University Press, 1993).

Rozemond, Marleen, *Descartes's Dualism* (Cambridge: Harvard University Press, 1998).

Shea, William R., *The Magic of Numbers and Motion: The Scientific Career of René Descartes* (Canton, MA: Science History Publications, 1991).

Thijssen-Schoute, Caroline, *Nederlands cartesianisme* (Amsterdam, 1954).

The Treasury of the Encyclopedia Britannica, ed. Clifton Fadiman (New York: Viking, 1992).

Verbeek, Theo (ed.), *La Querelle d'Utrecht* (Paris: Les impressions nouvelles, 1988).

Wittgenstein, Ludwig, *Culture and Value* (Oxford: Blackwell, 1980).

name index

Lethe, 63
Levi, Anthony, 144, 147
Loeb, Louis E., 140
Lucretius, 91
Luynes, duc de, 46

Malebranche, Nicolas, 113
Mersenne, Marin, 3, 3–4, 6–7, 8, 11, 14, 43, 56, 58, 63, 72–3, 76, 79, 136, 140, 141
Mesland, 87, 89
Molière, 5, 72, 74, 91, 141, 146
Molina, Tirso de, 138, 140
Morus, 11, 136
Moyal, George, 137, 147
Mozart, Wolfgang Amadeus, 48, 72

Newcastle, Marquess of, 43, 44, 46, 136
Nietzsche, Friedrich Wilhelm, 2, 87, 146

Paracelsus, 140, 146
Plantinga, Alvin, 138, 147

Plato, 2, 19, 27, 52, 71, 89, 107, 120, 146
Pollot, Alphonse, 44, 136

Regius, 4, 9, 11, 89, 101, 108, 114, 115, 140, 142, 143
Rochemonteix, Camille de, 63, 146
Rousseau, Jean-Jacques, 76, 141, 146
Rozemond, Marleen, 138, 143, 147

Shea, William R., 136, 147
Silhon, 138
Spinoza, Baruch, 93, 113, 141, 146
Strindberg, August, 23
Suárez, Francisco, 19, 20, 137, 146

Thijssen-Shoute, Caroline, 137, 147
Titania, 93, 94–5

Ulysses, 72

Verbeek, Theo, 142, 147

Wittgenstein, Ludwig, 2, 119, 120, 143, 147

subject index